CULTURE
FIX

CULTURE FIX

HOW TO CREATE A GREAT PLACE TO WORK

FIX

COLIN D ELLIS

WILEY

First published in 2020 by John Wiley & Sons Australia, Ltd
42 McDougall St, Milton Qld 4064

Office also in Melbourne

Typeset in 12pt/14.5pt Adobe Caslon Pro

© John Wiley & Sons Australia, Ltd 2020

The moral rights of the author have been asserted

ISBN: 978-0-730-37149-6

A catalogue record for this book is available from the National Library of Australia

Cover design by Wiley

Index by Don Jordan, Antipodes Indexing

10 9 8 7 6 5 4 3 2 1

Disclaimer

The material in this publication is of the nature of general comment only, and does not represent professional advice. It is not intended to provide specific guidance for particular circumstances and it should not be relied on as the basis for any decision to take action or not take action on any matter which it covers. Readers should obtain professional advice where appropriate, before making any such decision. To the maximum extent permitted by law, the author and publisher disclaim all responsibility and liability to any person, arising directly or indirectly from any person taking or not taking action based on the information in this publication.

For J, T & C x

CONTENTS

FOREWORD

Like Colin, I've always felt that culture makes all the difference. Now I'm at Atlassian, an organisation famous for its culture (and winner of multiple 'best place to work' awards), that feeling has become a certain knowledge. I know the importance of a strong, evolving culture for successfully scaling a business. Culture, or to put it simply, the way your people act when you *aren't* there, is a force multiplier for your business. An open, empowered, high-trust, collaborative culture of cognitive diversity will enable your business to thrive.

The best leaders in the world recognise that culture isn't something you pick up on PowerPoint; it's not something a consultant sells you or a poster in the office tea room. It's a set of behaviours that you role model as a leader and inspire in those around you.

Colin's fresh approach to getting under the surface of culture, understanding the cause and effect, confronting some of the uncomfortable truths, and owning up to some of the honest mistakes, is very refreshing.

This book brings you loads of practical insights, while pleading with you to take action. It will make you laugh, and maybe even inwardly cry a little, as you observe the anti-patterns in action. It will inspire you to take ownership of your leadership style, your team's success and your organisation's evolution. It will provoke you to unlearn old habits that won't work in the future, and to step bravely into experimentation and exploration. It will guide you towards ownership, accountability and not being a passenger. It will equip you with everything you need to be the best version of yourself.

Colin also draws on the thinking of some of the best minds in business. Using this book as a guide, you can become a great leader every day, building a culture that you, your people and your customers embrace with enthusiasm and that everyone else aspires to.

Underline key passages. Fold back the corners of pages. Take notes. Highlight sections. Share stories. Just promise me one thing: after you've read this book, don't just sit there and nod — take your new-found courage and *do something different*. And don't be quiet about it.

If, as is true here at Atlassian, people are your biggest asset, your role is to create an environment where they feel like they belong, and where they know they can do the best job of their life, every single day.

Dom Price
Work Futurist, Atlassian
Sydney, 2019

PREFACE

Speaking of the literature on management, in *Creativity Inc.* Ed Catmull said, 'The books I read that promised insight on the topic were mostly devoid of content.' One of the books on culture I read while researching this book declared on its first page, 'We do not offer here a series of checklists or a "how to" manual.' No one ever does.

I was once told that writing a 'how to' book would kill my cultural evolution business. As an aspiring manager 20 years ago, though, the thing I wanted to read *more than anything* was a book that spelled out not only what good team-building and culture looked like, but how to do it really well. Given that our success depended on it, it seemed ridiculous to me that such a book didn't exist.

I have attended my fair share of utterly soul-destroying team-building workshops, chock full of games and icebreakers that I was assured would be 'fun'. They weren't, and they contributed nothing to building a culture that lasted beyond the day.

That's not to say there aren't some good culture books out there. There are some really good ones—you'll find a list of the ones I've read (and have quoted from) at the end of this book. It's just that none of them gave me the information I needed back then to go and do it myself.

So I've attempted to write a 'how to' book, and hope you'll join me at the impending funeral for my business. I've started work on the eulogy, just in case.

You can read the book in any order you like. Front to back is conventional, but some sections will look more interesting than others, so you just go right ahead and jump around as you see fit. That said, I've tried to frame it in a way that makes logical sense and will be most practically useful to readers who are trying to establish a new culture or fix an existing one.

At some stage, though, you'll probably find yourself thinking something like this: 'Jeez, this sounds hard. There's no way we could do that in our company [or school, sports team, hospital etc.].'

If I had a dollar for every time I'd heard a client say something like this, I'd have $62.50 now (I had to cut someone off mid-sentence once). It's a classic case of fixed mindset thinking. People talk about culture as being the most important thing, but they look for every possible way to avoid doing it, because—like most things—it involves risk, time and money. Instead, they back quick-fix interventions, which may provide short-term impetus but offer nothing in the way of long-term change or growth.

So as you start to read this, I'd ask you to resist the lure of the fixed mindset and instead focus on how you can take the examples and activities presented here and apply them to your culture.

You're not and never will be Netflix (unless you're an employee of Netflix, in which case *you* are), so stop trying to be someone else and instead focus on the steps you need to take to build a better version of the culture you have now. Think big, but start small.

There'll be things in here you disagree with, and that's awesome! But rather than conform to the current social disease of being an armchair critic, be an armchair inspiration and share what worked for you instead, because you never know, it might just work for someone else too.

Oh and there's just no way this book can provide you with all the answers to all the culture questions for your team or organisation, in your industry, at this moment in time. I hope, though, it will provide you with the base information and the inspiration to go away and find the rest of the answers you need.

STOP TALKING AND START DOING

One of the first things I do when I start working with different cultures around the world is to get them to *stop talking about culture*, particularly leaders. When you talk about it endlessly but don't take any real action, people stop caring—and that's if they cared to begin with! It starts to be seen as a fad and something that executives feel like they *should* be talking about.

A survey of almost 1400 American businesses found that a whopping 92 per cent of senior executives cited cultural change as a critical driver to increase their company's values, yet a paltry 16 per cent said their culture 'is exactly where it should be'.

Conversely, there's also a real danger that when leaders talk obsessively about the culture they've created, it can be seen as an object of veneration and devotion. Take the 'ure' out of culture and you have a cult; take the 'Ure' out of Ultravox and you have … well, nothing really. Gen-X jokes aside (and steel yourself for a few more of those), turning into a cult might lead to the loss of the people who created it or put off the very people you're trying to attract.

I do not address the differences in social cultures and have tried to remain agnostic on that, which as you can imagine is quite difficult. As I mention in other places in the book, if you're looking for information on how to work differently with other cultures around the world, then books such as

The Culture Map by Erin Meyer will provide much more information. I have, however, provided some examples of things to think about from my own experiences that will encourage you to take a different approach or to seek out more information. And Jodie (my fantastic business manager and co-researcher) and I have tried to find case studies from all kinds of cultures to demonstrate that it's not just the technology giants of Silicon Valley who do it well.

It will become apparent that I like the way certain organisations (mainly technology ones, as they put the most time and effort into it) do things more than others. I like these organisations because they make culture easy to do and this is why people enjoy working, learning and playing there. These organisations are also great at sharing *how* they do it, and the things I share in the book barely scratch the surface of what they've put in the public domain. So I urge you to go and do your own research. Just don't overdo it. As Jason Fried and David Hannemeir Hanson point out in their book *ReWork*, 'Too much academia can do you harm.' Collect just enough information to take action, then get to it—don't become a content vacuum.

This book is written for cultures of all sizes. It works for classrooms, football offensive units and retail stores. However, for the vision to be achieved it needs to be tied to the overall organisational culture and the other subcultures. You probably already have elements of the culture you're looking for in some of your subcultures, so it's important that you get them to share what they're doing well so others can learn.

AND FINALLY...

By the time you read this, there's a very real possibility that at least one of the organisations I feature has gone bust or been rocked by scandal, its shocking cultural practices exposed, its leaders indicted for the lies they've told or the emotional and physical distress they've caused others. What can I say? All I can tell you is that right now, as I'm writing this on my balcony in the Australian summer heat of early 2019, none of this has happened. I promise I'll make all necessary corrections in future editions.

Throughout the book I refer to cultures rather than teams, classes, cohorts, squads or any similar colloquialism. Whether you're an educational establishment, religious group, engineering organisation or sports team, your culture is what you do.

So that's it. If you enjoy this book, pass it on. Knowledge of how to improve is the gift that keeps on giving. But don't consume it then do nothing with it. Knowledge is important, but only when you take action.

Colin
Melbourne, 2019

THE
CULTURE
CHALLENGE

WHAT IS CULTURE?

There is nothing more important to any organisation than its culture. In his 2017 Letter to Shareholders, Amazon's Jeff Bezos explained, 'Building a culture of high standards is well worth the effort, and there are many benefits. Naturally and most obviously, you're going to build better products and services for customers—this would be reason enough!' According to accounting firm Deloitte, 'Building a Future Focused Culture' is the number one priority for global organisations, yet only 19 per cent claim they have the 'right' culture for success.

Culture permeates absolutely everything an organisation is and does, from the behaviour of senior leaders in large global companies to the way a sports team trains for a game at the weekend. It dictates where people sit in a classroom, how meetings are run in an office, how decisions are made on a ship, how construction projects are delivered, how orchestras play together and how clothes are marketed online.

Culture is the thing that gets people out of bed in the morning and is often the last thing people think of before they go to bed at night. It brings people together and tears them apart. It generates optimism and can make or break a weekend or holiday.

When the culture is vibrant it's something you want to be part of, whether you work in it or not. It's not limited to winning teams, Ivy League universities or technology titans. In a coffee shop, hair salon, design agency, doctors surgery or lecture theatre you can sense it, feel it and touch it. It's infectious, intoxicating and electric. You ponder what it would be like to work there. You see the smile on people's faces, hear the music they're playing or the conversations they're having. You want to create a great place to work for yourself.

Stagnant cultures are equally noticeable. There's little interaction between people, no laughter or human noise. It feels cold, lost, and you want to get away from there as soon as possible.

Culture is not 'owned' by anyone, as everyone gets a say in culture. A People and Culture department, teacher or team manager may be the custodian of culture, but they don't get to pin a tail on it and say it's theirs.

Wherever you sit on an organisational chart, whatever your length of service or performance, you get a say in the culture, because culture is the totality of everyone's behaviours, stories, beliefs, traditions, skills and habits.

A large corporate organisation can employ a firm of consultants to come in and work with the senior management team to define the culture, but this exercise will fail because (a) the consultants aren't part of the culture; (b) the staff who work within the culture every day can (rightly) reject it as not being something they agree with; and (c) the whole exercise is often undermined by the fact that senior leaders don't change their own behaviours to demonstrate that this is different from what's gone before.

While senior managers don't own culture, they have the power to destroy it through their actions or inactions. This is the dichotomy of culture for those who own businesses. They know it's important, and they want to do something about it, but by doing nothing, or by doing the wrong thing, it gets worse and results continue to suffer.

* * *

This is true of sports teams that persist with a manager when the players have rejected the culture. It's true of an engineering company where one person's behaviour undermines the work of others. It's true of organisations whose leaders act unethically and expect others to do likewise. Recent examples such as those at Enron and Volkswagen are testament to this.

There's a growing recognition of culture's importance because there are more and more books and blogs that talk about it. But too often the response is to assume that changing it is too hard and to look for quick-fix solutions instead. Implement a new way of working, tear down office walls, sell a star player, restructure a company or buy new equipment. All of these initiatives could benefit the culture in the long run, but they ignore the fact that culture is ultimately about the people in it right now.

As Daniel Coyle puts it in his book *The Culture Code*, 'Culture is a set of living relationships working toward a shared goal. It's not something you are. It's something you do.' Put another way, culture is teamwork. Get your teamwork right and you have a good culture. A good culture leads to happy people. Happy people feel empowered to make decisions and to do their best work. This work leads to good results. Good results benefit the staff and the company, and consequently lift the culture.

Conversely, get your teamwork wrong and you have a poor culture. A poor culture leads to unhappy people. Unhappy people don't feel empowered to make decisions and inertia sets in. Targets are missed and opportunities are lost. Good staff leave and the culture suffers.

BUT WHERE TO START?

'About 700,000 years ago,' writes Yuval Noah Harari in his book *Sapiens*, 'organisms belonging to the species Homo Sapiens started to form even more elaborate structures called cultures. The subsequent development of these human cultures is called history.' It's important to start with the very thing that keeps cultures together and drives them apart. People.

To point out that people are at the heart of everything is to state the obvious, right? Of course, cultures are about people, you say. Who else could they be about? But if it's so obvious, then why does so much cultural activity not involve people? People often don't get to choose their favoured way of working or get asked for their opinions on the way things should be done. Their hours are dictated, their leaders chosen for them.

It never used to be this way. Early humans did pick their leaders. They selected the strongest, bravest person to lead the tribe, organise them into groups to hunt and protect them from danger. These leaders created followers, who wanted to emulate the leader. If the leader was strong and aggressive, the tribe would be likewise. If the leader was kind and empathetic, the tribe would reflect this. If the leader was weak and the tribe went hungry or was put in danger, then the tribe would kill him. Hey, that's early humans for you!

The same is true of today's business leaders. Without the killing, obviously. If there's an aggressive and bullying leader, there's a good chance their team will copy that behaviour. Same with a kind and empathetic leader. Organisations with weak leadership tend to tolerate and excuse it.

In the past we were far more subservient as employees. As a 17-year-old entering the workforce in 1987 I was told to keep my head down and do as I was told and I'd be fine. So that's what I did. Until I didn't get a decision I needed, didn't get help when I had too much on my plate or wasn't granted development to ensure that I could do the job to the best of my ability. At that point, I lifted my head up and started asking questions of my teammates, manager and (where I didn't get the response I was looking for) *their* manager. At that point, I was influencing the culture of the organisation.

Still, back in 1987 I could be told—quite forcefully—to be quiet and do my job. Empathy really wasn't a thing that was done consistently. When it *was* done, it was a breath of fresh air and almost everyone within the culture responded to it.

The workforce of 2019 and beyond—regardless of which generation they were born into—expect empathy by default. We're more attuned to our emotions than ever before and we want to be part of an experience that inspires and motivates us, one that we can talk about positively.

In offices and classrooms we're using digital tools to inform, support and replace the work we do. These tools often lie at the centre of transformation programs. IDC Group estimates that global spending on digital transformation alone will exceed US$2.1 trillion by 2021. This money will transform the way students learn, doctors diagnose, teams build and organisations work.

But the tools alone don't transform anything. After all, as my friend Dom Price says, 'a fool with a tool is still a fool'.

What digital transformation requires above all else is for the people using the new tools (or ways of working) to think and act differently. Not to have, in the words of Dr Carol Dweck, a *fixed mindset* about what's possible or what's gone before, but to have a *growth mindset* that talks of opportunity and is curious by nature.

Understanding the mindset that individuals are adopting at a particular point in time is a key facet of what it means to be self-aware. People who lack self-awareness and who resist change and being part of these new ways of doing things will hold back culture, digital or otherwise, and results will suffer.

A 2017 McKinsey report noted, 'The narrow, parochial mentality of workers who hesitate to share information or collaborate across functions and departments can be corrosive to organizational culture.' A first sign of this is a lack of trust between teammates. In a culture without trust bad behaviours are rife, decision making is poor, poor performance is excused and the ability of people to work together—or collaborate—is undermined. One study in 2017 reported that 78 per cent of staff interviewed said they didn't trust their teammates.

This kind of environment encourages more rules and less autonomy. The worst of people is anticipated and people start to leave in droves. Good people, that is. The bad ones, the ones whose poor behaviours include favouring individual glory over collaboration, stay on to ensure that all future cultural change is frustrated.

And this attrition costs money, lots of money. The US Bureau of National Affairs found in 2017 that US$11 billion is lost in this way annually. And all because organisations don't take the time to continually define and evolve 'the way we do things around here'.

MONEY ALONE CAN'T FIX CULTURE

After getting US$150 million in VC funding from (PayPal co-founder) Peter Thiel in 2012, Airbnb CEO Brian Chesky asked him what was the single most importance piece of advice he had for them as a business. Thiel replied, 'Don't fuck up the culture.'

What Thiel was warning against was the age-old practice of investing in quick-fix cultural solutions. Got some money to spend on culture? Here are some great ideas:

- Throw money at people to show them how much they're valued.

- Change the office space to make it easier to collaborate.

- Buy lots of new tools to show staff you're on the cutting edge of technology.

- Send everyone on a training course on the latest method of working.

These all look like good things to do to improve the culture and loyalty of your people, yet not one of them will do so on its own. Sure, you may get some short-term gains, but they'll be just that—short-term.

As Chesky himself commented, 'Culture is a thousand things, a thousand times.' Yes, it requires money and time, but they are useless if people don't have a mindset that supports the need to continually evolve and the commitment to actually make it happen.

Commitment to culture from senior management can be demonstrated in different ways. Richard Branson's commitment is one of empathy and fun. Elon Musk's commitment is one of risk-taking and big goals. Steve Jobs was about quality and exceeding expectations. In reality, it needs to encompass all of these things and be wrapped up in humanistic behaviour that is respectful and that communicates in a way that the people receiving the information appreciate and feel able to provide feedback on.

When we talk about 'buy-in', what we mean is commitment to the cause. This commitment is driven by culture. Does the team understand what it has to achieve? Does it have what it needs to support the achievement of these goals? Does the leader ensure that equality exists? Is poor performance and behaviour dealt with? Is the communication tailored to the individual? Are opportunities to grow and develop inherent? Is the 'system' easy to use? Are there opportunities for people to get to know each other better?

INPUT AND OUTPUT CULTURE MODELS

To continually build an environment that's fit for purpose for any type of organisation to achieve its goals, it's vital that culture be the number one investment and not something that's just talked about in boardrooms, classrooms or dressing rooms. It's more important than that.

For example, a retail company whose clothing line isn't selling as expected needs to look at all elements of its culture. Do they understand what their customers are looking for?

Are their clothes on-trend? Are they priced appropriately? Are they easy to buy? Are the stores welcoming? Are the staff polite and helpful? Do the corporate processes allow for quick decisions? Do staff feel empowered? Are budgets sufficient? Are new ideas welcomed?

Every single one of these things exists within a culture. No wonder it feels hard to change! 'It wasn't like Spotify was this amazing idea from day one,' Daniel Ek, its CEO, points out. 'It has evolved.'

The input model

The six pillars that support the culture are:

1. Personality & communication

2. Vision

3. Values

4. Behaviour

5. Collaboration

6. Innovation.

The way into any culture is through the personality of its people and how they communicate with each other. The culture centres on an aspirational vision and strong values, which in turn influence both strategy and goals. Crucial to achieving the vision are the way people behave, and how they work together and make time for new ideas.

Underneath these pillars are nine fundamentals that provide structure to those cultures that require it. In autonomous vibrant cultures these fundamentals are not as prevalent. For example, Spotify's Code of Conduct and Ethics contains just three bullet points:

• Do the right thing.

• Be nice.

• Play fair.

A similar code of one government agency I used to work for ran to 34 pages. The excuse I hear always centres on the different expectations of private sector vs government/public money, and while there may be an element of truth in that, I know from my own experience that the cultures in government agencies are often driven by self-serving bureaucrats looking to make things more complicated than they need to be.

All of the components contained within the input model below must be addressed by the people within a culture so they have what they need to be able to do their best work. Should any of these elements be missing or underinvested in, then the culture will suffer.

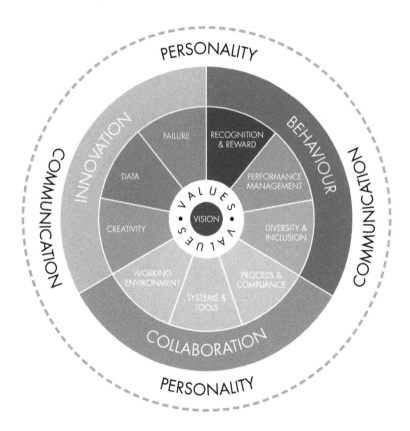

This book covers all of the actions you need to take to ensure that each component of the input model is addressed.

The output model

The culture output is determined by the efforts, mindset, behaviours and engagement of those belonging to a culture in applying the inputs. If each is continuously assessed and people behave in accordance with the agreement they have made, then the output is likely to be a vibrant culture. If they aren't addressed and behaviours are poor, then the culture will stagnate.

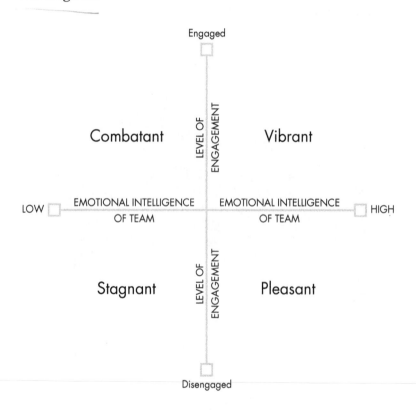

The output model is built around two axes:

1. The emotional intelligence of the team

Self-aware individuals, suggest Marcus Buckingham and Curt Coffman in their book *First, Break All The Rules: What the World's Greatest Managers Do Differently*, 'are the building blocks of great teams'. Self-aware people are much more likely to be able to recognise and manage their own emotions.

This emotional intelligence (EQ) has been undervalued and underinvested in for too long.

Traditionally, academic qualifications were understood as the single most essential attribute for an employee, yet this often didn't play out in teams where it wasn't required. Psychologist Daniel Goleman found that 'at best IQ contributes about 20% to the factors that determine life success, which leaves 80% to other forces'. EQ forms a large part of this 80 per cent.

Goleman wrote the book on emotional intelligence and categorically proved its value to teams around the world.

Researcher Peter Salovey further broke down emotional intelligence into five domains:

- knowing one's emotions—self-awareness
- managing those emotions—handling feelings
- motivating oneself—marshalling emotions
- recognising emotions in others—empathy
- handling relationships—social competence.

Each of these domains is critical to an individual's contribution to a vibrant team culture.

2. The level of engagement

Engagement is one of those words dreamt up by unimaginative people—you know, the ones who also brought you, well, *human resources*. In a cultural context it actually relates to how interested you are in the success of what you're doing. Like emotional intelligence, engagement needs to be addressed at both a personal and group level.

For example, if a person is in a job they don't enjoy, then their engagement will be low, and we say 'they're pulling everyone else down with them'. The same is true of a team working towards something they don't believe they can achieve. They talk about their morale being at 'rock bottom' or 'on the floor'.

Lifting engagement requires purpose, clarity and dedication. If someone doesn't feel connected to something, then they have to be shown that the work they are doing is achievable and valuable, and that they have the support of the culture to get there.

Often a new hire can lose their engagement as soon as they walk through the door. If the manager and team are not there to greet them and make them feel welcome, then the enthusiasm built during the interview process is lost and it can take months to recover. By the same token, if on day one the team gather to welcome the new person, share a little of themselves, ensure they have everything they need to do their job and immediately include them in day-to-day activity, then their engagement is likely to be high. And not only theirs, for the team can gain a huge sense of satisfaction from making a new co-worker feel welcome.

The level of emotional intelligence and engagement dictates the culture at any given time.

Stagnant cultures are just 'meh'. No one really understands why they're doing what they're doing or even believes it can be done. There's no sense of teamwork and interaction is low. No one is pushing themselves or their teammates to be better at what they do, and there is a noticeable lack of energy and passion.

Signs of a stagnant culture include:

- apathy
- no visible communication / people avoidance
- lack of energy and passion
- 'hero' mentality
- consistently missed targets and deadlines
- no consequence for poor performance
- teams don't share their thoughts about what needs to change.

Pleasant cultures, on the other hand, are too nice. There is lots of intent, but it's often misplaced. Everyone pretends that everything is good, but privately they're not so sure. Group interactions are inefficient, and lots of time is spent talking about anything but the important issues to be addressed. There is lots of empathy, but also a sense that everything is hard to do.

Signs of a pleasant culture include:

- blind optimism
- lots of discussion but little action
- passive-aggressive communications
- low productivity
- contentedness with sub-par results or performances
- teams agreeing to disagree
- lots of emphasis on relationship building.

Combatant cultures are argumentative by nature. There are many unconstructive discussions that lead to heated debate and people become afraid to contribute. There's lots of infighting and backbiting and everything feels hard to do. Strong personalities insist their way is the right way and are unwilling to consider alternatives. High levels of sick or stress leave are common. Because engagement is high, plenty of action is taken; unfortunately it's often at the expense of the feelings of others.

Signs of a combatant culture include:

- using friction and hostility as a motivator
- progress 'despite' people
- low/no empathy
- raised voices and bad language
- gossip
- poor behaviours
- teams being told what to do.

Vibrant cultures are memorable. There is a buzz about them and you want to be part of what's being created. There's agreement on how they'll behave and work together. In times of crisis, rather than panic, there's resilience and resolve to collaborate to find a good solution. There's safety, open empathetic debate, social interaction, trust, empowerment, and a commitment to personal and group development. Good staff are retained, poor-performing staff are moved out and results are achieved.

Signs of a vibrant culture include:

- having agreed behaviours and cultural principles
- successes being celebrated
- failure being seen as learning
- inclusivity and diversity
- lots of social interaction
- continual investment in culture
- teams challenging each other to achieve their goals.

Whatever they do and wherever they are in the world, every kind of organisation will face cultural challenges at some stage. It's continual investment that will determine whether or not they survive. Over the past couple of years even mega-corporations such as Amazon, Walt Disney, Apple and Facebook have had high-profile culture issues, while transport innovator Uber continues to battle them almost daily. This thing called culture can't be fixed with band-aids or on a whim. It's a living, breathing embodiment of everything and everyone within the organisation.

THE VALUE OF CULTURE

So what is the value of culture? We're always being told it's the most important thing—and this book is no different in this regard—but what is the return on any investment in it? Most CEOs will want to know three things:

1. How long will it take?
2. How much will it cost?
3. What's the payback and when will I get it?

For years, those whose job it is to monitor culture have struggled with these questions. This has led to a lack of support for cultural change activity or, worse, apathy from the leadership team, because the payback was either hard to quantify or at odds with the investment of time and money.

In the age-old struggle of fast and cheap vs good, most organisations settle for the former and end up with solutions to problems they didn't have and with minimal payback.

Surveys, pulse checks, reviews and fact-finding missions on a culture usually provide feedback only on what needs to be fixed, not on the value loss. When I undertook these exercises myself using external organisations, what I found was an insistence that they camp in my department for months on end, thereby further undermining any value I would have got from their work. Worse still, they took the IP about cultural evolution with them, rather than instilling the activities or mindset into the people who need to do the work moving forward, because investing in culture is a medium- to long-term strategy, not a short-term one.

That means we need to abandon the concept of fast and cheap and focus instead on good.

Fast and cheap	Good
Executive-led culture definition	Staff-led cultural evolution
Annual appraisals	Continual feedback
New branding	More customer value
New ways of working	New ways of behaving
Tolerance of brilliant jerks	Managing out poorly behaved staff
Method implementation	Staff to select the way things need to be done
Training programs	Continuous learning
Process redesign	Process removal
Flexible working policy	'Design your own day'
Open plan offices	Mix of environments for different personalities
Table tennis tables	More time for free thinking and discussion

When this approach is taken, the value gained will be incremental initially, but after six to nine months (never sooner, in my experience), small things start to happen. Important team members no longer want to leave, confidence is higher, people are talking to each other, there's more laughter and more constructive discussion, and it *feels* different.

This is when your faith in the investment you've made in your culture is restored, yet too many organisations have thrown in the towel long before this and never get to see these shifts.

When I interviewed David D'Souza, Membership Director of the Chartered Institute of Personnel and Development (CIPD), in London I raised this issue. In his opinion, 'Organisations settle for the trappings—books, posters etc.—but you need to change the climate. Change people's day one day at a time so that in a year it feels like a completely different organisation.' He questioned the leadership of those who settle for fast and cheap. 'You're signing up either for a proper culture change program or for a shallow marketing one.'

One organisation I reference in the book is Dutch bank ING (Internationale Nederlanden Groep), who undertook a cultural evolution program in 2014–16. Their approach was not without pain, and they lost a significant number of people as they moved towards implementing a values-based culture that was more flexible in the way it delivered services. But net income rose from €2.7 billion in 2014 to €4.9 billion in 2017, and culture was a big part of that.

Financial growth is only one of the benefits of a strong culture. Depending on the type of culture you have, other benefits can include:

- improved communication
- greater productivity
- increased sales
- higher customer satisfaction
- increased likelihood of competitive achievement
- reduction in absenteeism
- retention of key staff/performers
- more ideas and innovation
- continual learning.

In its State of the American Workplace report of 2017, Gallup found that vibrant cultures produced:

- 17 per cent higher productivity overall
- 10 per cent higher customer satisfaction
- 20 per cent higher sales
- 21 per cent higher profitability
- 41 per cent lower absenteeism
- 59 per cent lower turnover
- 70 per cent fewer safety incidents
- 40 per cent fewer quality defects.

There is something here for every culture! However, it requires time, money and no shortage of effort to help employees to transition from one state to another. This creates a new level of happiness, which is when cultures get the biggest payback, because all the items listed above are only possible with happy staff. Happiness leads to accomplishment. This is the value of great culture.

In his book *Flow*, Mihaly Csikszentmihalyi comments, 'It seems clear that cultures differ from one another in terms of the degree of the "pursuit of happiness" they make possible.'

Those last three words are key here. Everyone within a culture has a responsibility, but it is the senior managers who make it possible by prioritising cultural activity, freeing up time to do different things, and spending money not only on the definition of it but also on its ongoing evolution.

BUILDING A CASE FOR CHANGE

In most organisations, if you want to spend money and time on any project, then a document has to be written, presented and approved before any work can start. As you'll see throughout this book, the great working cultures of the world don't hold themselves back in this way. They trust the intentions of their staff and support any work that will make employees happier, so everyone within the culture benefits.

In these cultures trust is assumed, not earned. The PwC CEO survey of 2017 found that 58 per cent of CEOs believe a lack of trust will harm business results, and they're right. Yet more often than not, this lack of trust comes directly from the boardroom.

Culture is expected to just happen, and when investment is requested CEOs wonder why. Why can't we just send everyone on a training course for the latest thing? Why can't we just go open plan?

Why can't we just rebrand?

These kinds of initiatives are seen as 'just another program' to put a sticking plaster over a gaping cultural wound. Worse still is when they're undertaken just before an engagement survey or in response to a consultant report.

I feel for consultants sometimes (not often, it has to be said; according to the *Wall Street Journal* they made US$63 billion in the US alone in 2017), as they're often called up by a senior management team to help change cultures. They're given the results of an engagement survey and told to come up with the answers. David D'Souza again: 'The idea that there's something out there called "culture" that if you could just get the right consultants in you can shape is wishful thinking at best and lazy thinking at worst.'

The fact is, staff will have been providing feedback on the culture both formally and informally for years, only for it to be ignored. They will have offered to fix things or requested time and money to do so, only to be told that there are more important things to do.

I sometimes feel that senior executives like to talk about culture but aren't prepared to take it on, preferring to stick to their 'it's hard to change' mantra in the hope that things will sort themselves out.

Following feedback from one of my clients on the program I run, I was approached by an organisation in 2017 to help them change their culture. We met twice and talked about the challenges they faced (high attrition rates, low engagement, bullying, poor performance, no clear priorities and so on). I helped them to develop the business case they needed to get CEO backing, and it sat in his inbox for six weeks. In the end the proposal was rejected because the CEO decided 'culture wasn't a priority for the organisation at the moment'.

Two years on and the organisation's performance is so bad that the CEO is regularly being called upon by the press to resign. He refuses to do so.

In complete contrast, I'm working with an organisation in Canberra, Australia, whose CEO named culture as his number one priority. He is leading by example and ensuring that his leadership team do likewise. They're encouraging staff, whether in the office or in the field, to challenge the little things they do on a regular basis in order to evolve the culture into something that every member of staff can be proud of.

It has some fantastic people leading the change in the subcultures (more on this in the next section), and almost every week there is a different initiative being undertaken in a different part of the organisation.

It's a big commitment of time and money, and some people who don't want to be part of the new culture or whose values don't match those the organisation wants to embrace have already left. In just four months, however, engagement has already improved, confidence is high and it's starting to 'feel different from before'.

CULTURAL EVOLUTION STARTS WITH A LONE NUT

My favourite TED talk is a three-minute masterpiece from Derek Sivers. Behind him is a grainy, shaky video of a shirtless guy who seems to be making a fool of himself by dancing at a music festival, on his own, in the middle of a field. But, as Sivers points out, this guy believes 100 per cent in what he's doing. He's at a music festival—why wouldn't he dance? The fact that no one else is dancing doesn't matter to him, neither does the fact that he has no dancefloor. The one thing you definitely do at a music festival—speaking from experience here—is dance.

So he has guts and courage to stand out from everyone else. Every time someone joins him, he embraces them as equals. These followers then embrace the new followers as equals and within the space of two minutes the whole field is dancing with the shirtless dancing guy. As Sivers skilfully points out, the first follower is the person who turns the lone nut into a leader!

And what cultural change and evolution requires to be successful is a lone nut. Someone who is going to stand out from the crowd and do things differently. Someone who has different ideas and believes in creating energy through shared stories and experience, while still ensuring that the 'work' gets done. It might be the CEO, as is the case with the organisation I'm working with in Canberra, but it could just as easily be a team leader or someone else who is managing a small subculture within the organisation.

These are the people whose conversations, meetings and training sessions are different. Whose methods are tailored to individuals, who can converse with all levels of people, who celebrate success, actively manage poor performance and make you feel that anything is possible.

They are role models in every sense of the word and set the example for others to follow. They are people who take the time to listen, to grow and to work closely with their staff to remove barriers and inspire incredible performance from those around them. People like Marie Curie, Herb Kelleher, Sheryl Sandberg, Sir Alex Ferguson, Katrina Adams, Aarti Shah and Ben Zander.

People like this are a positive driving force for change. They are empathetic when it would be easier to be dismissive. They make time for new ideas and thinking. People want to be around them, because they know they are worth following. They have a tractor beam that you're drawn to and you know they won't allow themselves to get dragged to the dark side.

Leonardo Da Vinci put it best when he said, 'It has long since come to my attention that people of accomplishment rarely sat back and let things happen to them. They went out and happened to things.'

Leading any kind of cultural initiative can't be done part-time. It can't be dropped after three months. It's not an isolated series of posters, marketing statements or press releases. It's people with the determination to be lone nuts, to positively challenge the status quo and to embrace every follower as an equal. You won't all be dancing shirtless in a field, but the feeling will be the same.

The starting point for any cultural evolution program is to ensure that those who 'own' the investment in it fully understand the value of the work ahead, the positives and negatives of the change and the senior management commitment to it. They need to know there are no rules for management that are different from the rules for everyone else and that all issues, concerns and suggestions for improvement will be considered and acted on.

Ultimately it's the people on the ground who will have to do the most work, so their commitment must be high for the culture to become what it aspires to be.

Simply telling them that culture is the most important thing or that change is the norm won't gain their buy-in, neither will telling them to be positive about it. This approach always makes me laugh when I hear it. Like all it takes to turn someone's attitude around is to tell them to be more optimistic! You can't tell someone to be positive about culture change; you have to show them and then keep showing them and when they do exhibit behaviours in line with the organisation's values, then you thank them for their efforts.

Then maybe (and it's only a *maybe* in the early days) they start to feel more positive. If, however, you stop doing the things you said you would, then all the trust that had been gained and was starting to be assumed is lost and the culture is back where it was when the initiative started.

It's really that simple and can happen that quickly. Don't become another failed culture change statistic. Get people involved, set expectations well, keep communicating and above all never forget that you're dealing with human beings.

CASE STUDY: HSBC, Argentina

One of my favourite cultural evolution case studies is from HSBC in Argentina back in 2009. At that time, the organisation had multiple cultures, and had recently completed a downsizing exercise, a merger and a massive systems integration. It was the perfect storm of cultural challenges and a new 'way of doing things' had to be established.

They developed a program to provide every single one of their 6000 employees with the knowledge of what it takes to be a leader. It wasn't restricted to senior managers or selected individuals. It was offered to everyone, because as then CEO Antonio Losada said, 'I do not believe that true change can be done by a small group of people, regardless of their level of commitment or insight.'

All attendees were then invited to make changes to add value wherever they could. They weren't required to ask for permission to do so; they were given free rein to engage others and change the smallest of things.

In less than three months, the culture had started to evolve and they were able to realise:

- improved collaboration
- improved customer relationships
- increased sales
- reduced operating costs.

'Instead of focusing energy and resources on theories, models and labels,' explained culture evolution partner Javier Bajer, 'HSBC Argentina engaged the entire organisation in changing its culture through the application of tens of thousands of specific and individual actions.'

KEY POINTS

- The case for change has to be easy to understand and well communicated.
- You can't tell people to be positive — you have to show them.
- Strong leadership and commitment to the evolution are required.

ACTION YOU CAN TAKE

When building a case for cultural evolution, ensure you take into consideration the feedback from staff, as this is often ignored in favour of financials centred on reducing operational costs or increasing productivity.

While these are important, gaining buy-in from those within the culture means convincing them that this isn't just another senior management initiative to reduce costs or do more for less. That this is different and includes provision for time to prioritise work, come up with new ideas, celebrate success and challenge the things within the culture that are holding it back.

Give them the opportunity to contribute to the case for change by inviting submissions on the things they'd like to see. An engagement survey could be used to do this, but better still would be a series of roadshows or workshops that set out the cultural evolution agenda and that invite immediate and creative feedback to be incorporated into the case for change.

CULTURES & SUBCULTURES

One term I hear a lot, mostly in a negative context, is the word 'silo'. It's used to describe either functional or dysfunctional *subcultures* within an overall organisational culture. Highly productive silos can in fact be a very good thing, but only providing they work and communicate well with other highly productive silos. Otherwise the organisation will suffer and these subcultures will be seen as outliers.

It's vitally important in larger organisational cultures that time and effort is put into developing each subculture, then ensuring that the bonds between these subcultures are strong. The four types of cultures—Stagnant, Pleasant, Combatant and Vibrant—can exist at all levels of an organisation and the vibrancy of an organisation's overall culture is determined by the strength of its subcultures.

A school may have a vibrant English department but a stagnant science department. The overall school culture will tend to feel pleasant as a result, as it's good in some areas but not in others.

Teachers have a huge (and unenviable) job of keeping multiple personalities engaged and creating a classroom where they can be the best version of themselves. If they drop the ball for just five minutes, then the culture (as determined by the students) can quickly become stagnant and they have to 'pick everyone up again'.

In the movie *Dead Poets Society*, Robin Williams' character, teacher John Keating, did just this by creating an anti-establishment subculture that challenged students to think and act differently from the rest of the school. In true Hollywood style Keating proved his mettle as a leader of change and remained true to his values. His style, however, was completely at odds with the command and control culture of the school. His hiring was seen as a failure of the school leadership and he was promptly fired. I won't reveal why, just in case you haven't seen the movie.

General Stanley McChrystal, in his book *Team of Teams: New Rules of Engagement for a Complex World*, talks about the same thing. Tasked with leading American special operations soldiers in the pursuit of Al Qaeda in Iraq, what he found was a series of groups that were efficient but simply didn't know how to work with one another. '[E]ach team exhibited horizontal bonds of trust and a common sense of purpose, but the only external ties that mattered to each team ran vertically. Meaningful relationships between teams were nonexistent.'

The goals of the mission were clear, but the way teams operated *together* was not.

Nowhere is this problem more evident than with major projects in large corporate organisations. According to PwC, more than US$78 trillion is expected to be spent on capital and infrastructure projects worldwide between 2014 and 2025, yet most research shows that project success rates sit at around 35 per cent or lower. Project Management Institute research estimates that almost US$1 million is wasted on projects every 20 seconds!

Projects are subcultures of the overall organisational culture. It doesn't matter whether you're building a stadium, laying track, implementing a technology system or introducing a new school curriculum.

Each project subculture requires definition to ensure that it not only defines the outcomes by which it will measure its success, but also provides its people with the opportunity to define *how* they will work together to deliver it. This almost never happens. Projects rush headlong into planning and delivery without any thought of defining the culture, then they wonder why it all turns to custard halfway through.

Projects are just one example. Every large organisation, regardless of what it does, is broken into subcultures. American football teams establish offence and defence subcultures, while baseball has batting and pitching ones. Retail organisations have subcultures in each store as well as at head office. And in the head offices themselves there are subcultures around People, Technology, Procurement and so on.

In my experience, as soon as you have six or more people working together on something, it's important to establish formal 'rules of engagement' for this subculture to ensure their vision for themselves and what they have to achieve links up with the overall organisational vision. This will ensure that the cultural expectations are set *before* work starts without having to fix it when promises are broken or targets missed.

This can then be shared with other subcultures to enhance relationships, create collaborative working practices, reduce the risk of duplication and bring understanding to how everyone will contribute to the success of the organisation.

There should never be any hidden agendas or 'mine is better than yours' when it comes to subcultures. There should be healthy competition driving everyone towards a common goal. This is something that software company Atlassian are very good at. Teams within the organisation compete against each other but in a highly productive way. I've been fortunate to spend some time in their Sydney office, and from my interactions with them I always feel that the staff work *with* the organisation, not *for* it, and that the best way they can do this is by pushing each other forward. They put team success first and individual success second.

This is what healthy subcultures look like.

Every manager, regardless of where they are in an organisation, has to become great at building vibrant subcultures. All too often we assume this is a skill people will have because they've been part of a team themselves, but this is not always the case. Once learned, however, it can never be unlearned. It just requires some regular maintenance and updating to ensure it always remains fit for purpose and the future of work.

DISTRIBUTED TEAMS

At the time of writing, Atlassian have 450 teams across their 3000 employees in eight locations around the world. Most of the offices in which these people work have access to the same technology and tools. Teams based in different Atlassian offices but working on the same things are called distributed teams.

Of crucial importance to a distributed team is that they agree on rituals (culture) at the start of a piece of work so everyone understands *how* it is going to be delivered. Often they will fly to a central location to agree on this. Where the opportunity exists to build relationships in person, they will take it, as it means they're much easier to maintain online.

Of course, this approach isn't cheap. It's a significant human investment that doesn't pay back immediately, but longer term it enhances relationships and leads to more productive conversations and decisions. This in itself improves the quality of the outcomes.

Where physical meetings are not possible they need a set of practices to facilitate virtual meetings. So they've developed a playbook to help them do this, and if you're thinking 'that sounds awesome!' the good news is they've made it publicly available. A quick Google search for Atlassian Team Playbook will take you there. It's a fantastic resource for bringing teams together in the right way.

Distributed teams all have access to tools such as Mural or Captivo, and use their own tools such as Confluence or Trello to track their work. They all see the same things and can share information in the same way. It's a setup that, once the rituals are agreed on, makes it easy to work together regardless of which office they are in.

REMOTE TEAMS

Remote teams, on the other hand, consist of people who work in environments where they don't have access to the same tools. They may use a video conferencing tool such as Meet, Zoom or Skype, but their ability to share other information using common tools is restricted.

It's still important to agree the culture up front, while recognising that everyone will have a different work environment.

There is often lots of suspicion around flexible and remote working, and I go into this in more detail under 'Working environment'. Suffice to say, it's important that cultures ensure they make it easy for their staff to create the right kind of environment to enable effective remote working.

This includes things such as ensuring that there's an agreement on the tools to be used and that laptops have them installed, and also ensuring that people have access to a good phone and internet service. Crucially, those working remotely need to have the discipline to get the job done in the same way they would in an office environment.

SUBCULTURES CAN TAKE MANY FORMS

Digital music service Spotify developed a unique set of subcultures that are broken down as follows:

- *Squads*—self-organising teams that sit together, set their own goals and priorities, and agree up front how they want to work together. They are 100 per cent responsible for the work they do.

- *Tribes*—multiple squads working in related areas. Each tribe is focused on delivering a specific set of features or objectives.

- *Chapters*—members of different squads who share knowledge, coach, mentor and develop one another's skills.

- *Guilds*—chapters that knowledge-share with other tribes.

If you've had to read this twice and think it sounds complicated, think again, because it works. Really well. So well in fact that cultures around the world are copying it relentlessly, whether it's appropriate for them to do so or not! Essentially, however, these are just self-organising, self-motivating subcultures within the larger Spotify culture.

Any organisation can do this. They don't have to use the same names, of course (although ING did just that for their cultural evolution program); they just have to acknowledge that subcultures exist in networks across a larger culture and that these subcultures start up and shut down at regular intervals to meet the changing requirements of this larger organisational network.

Truly remote teams also have to consider cultural and language barriers and collectively decide how they should best be overcome.

Erin Meyer is a professor at INSEAD (Institut Européen d'Administration des Affaires, or European Institute of Business Administration) and has spent years studying the differences in cultural work practices. Her book *The Culture Map* provides organisations with a guide on how to navigate the differences in customs and communication.

She says that working cultures frequently underestimate the challenges that come with diverse and remote teams, explaining, 'Effective cross-cultural collaboration can take more time than mono-cultural collaboration and often needs to be managed more closely.' She has also suggested, 'Cultural reality is the key to understanding the impact of culture on human interactions.'

This was brought home to me in the early 2000s when working with a development team in India. We thought we'd set the culture up in the right way. We spent time on video conference calls late in our day/early in theirs to get to know each other and established the culture we needed to be successful.

Our first mistake was to make the assumption that they worked in the same way we did: that where they weren't clear on something they would ask questions, that their working days lasted as long as ours did and that they would ensure decisions were made in a timely manner to ensure progress.

However, the Indian and UK cultures were quite different and where we were quite happy to ask for 'forgiveness not permission', that's not how they worked. They worked hierarchically and looked to a senior manager to tell them what to do, rather than making a decision and asking questions later.

We also didn't do enough to ensure that team success and cultural events were celebrated together, which led eventually to a completely avoidable 'us and them' situation.

I didn't make that mistake again.

About seven years later, we employed a development team from India to produce a crucial piece of work on behalf of the government agency in New Zealand I was working for. Here are some of the things we did:

- We flew the entire development team over from India for a two-day culture-building session—vision, personality, behaviours, innovation—followed by a series of planning sessions. Throughout this week we dined together in the evenings to understand more about the working practices and culture in Mumbai.

- We celebrated Diwali and they celebrated Waitangi Day (a New Zealand national holiday).

- We celebrated success via video conference and ensured that their managers gave praise when the agreed behaviours were demonstrated, and that poor performance was managed.

- We used electronic tools to stay connected and changed working hours so we were better able to work together.

- We had a 'phone first, email last' policy to ensure 'lost in translation' issues were minimised.

- We looked everywhere within our culture—regardless of role or location—for ideas that could enhance what we were doing.

Our approach worked. Our incredibly tight deadlines for delivery were met, and of course we celebrated that success in multiple locations around the world! This highly efficient cross-cultural subculture became the role model for similar programs in other departments.

Defining the vision and values at an organisational level are the first steps in building a vibrant working culture. However, it's only when the teams within that culture do likewise that you reap the value. It only takes one bad subculture to pull the rest of the organisation down. That can't be allowed to happen.

CASE STUDY: Manchester United

Football team Manchester United are a good example of how to utilise a strong subculture to influence and change the overall organisational culture. A club steeped in tradition, they were immensely successful in the 1950s and 1960s, but during the 1970s and 1980s had seen their fortunes wane. In 1986 they appointed a new manager and gave him the opportunity to rebuild the culture of the club.

Alex Ferguson set about creating not only a first team capable of winning trophies, but also a strong scouting and youth system to ensure talent continually flowed into the squad. The team had moderate success in the early days of Ferguson's tenure, then managed to win the English Premier League championship in 1992–93 and again in 1993–94.

Below the first team squad was a youth team who were highly motivated to succeed, drove each other's performance and mixed socially off the pitch, and they swept all before them at youth level.

Having failed to win the Premier League in 1994–95, the manager decided to leverage the subculture created in the youth team and promote six of them to the first team.

It didn't start well. The younger players were abruptly thrown into a very different culture and it took a while for them to exert their influence on it, leaving one misguided pundit to declare that 'you can't win anything with kids'. Nine months later they had lifted two domestic trophies including the championship, and set the club on a course to become the most successful ever in British football.

Many sporting teams build these kinds of youth subcultures that plant the seeds for the future, but very few allow them to grow into trees.

KEY POINTS

- Vibrant organisational cultures are the sum of their subcultures.

- Where teams aren't co-located, shared rituals are needed to keep the subculture together.

- Globally remote teams require more work up front to ensure there are no communication issues.

ACTION YOU CAN TAKE

Rather than sending individuals on the latest process-heavy training program, invest instead in showing them how to create subcultures. It's a skill we often assume that everyone has, but they don't.

My own programs take two days, or find something that works best for you and your organisation. It should build on those programs that are already offered and include exercises that are relevant for the age in which we live now.

Old-fashioned team-building days or off-sites should be avoided unless what's being covered is unlike anything you have ever done before. It should feel challenging for some, but ultimately everyone will have the same knowledge of what it takes to build and maintain subcultures.

I list a number of books at the back of this book that will provide valuable insights into how others have done it.

THE SIX
PILLARS
OF CULTURE

PILLAR 1
PERSONALITY &
COMMUNICATION

The way into any culture is through its people. The more vibrant a culture, the more its people open its doors, roll out the welcome mat and make new people feel part of it. The less vibrant the culture, the more its people either have to force their way into it or are left on the outside, wondering what it will take to get an invitation to join.

The behaviours of an individual in cultures is driven by:

- how self-aware they are
- how self-aware others around them are.

It's the capacity to be self-aware that allows people to understand the things they're good at, the things they need to work on and how to utilise the feedback they receive in order to continue to grow as a person.

The big problem, however, is that many people lack self-awareness and therefore cannot regulate their emotions, and consequently cultures never move forward. In her excellent book *Mindset: The New Psychology of Success*, Dr Carol Dweck notes, 'Studies showed that people are terrible at estimating their abilities. And those with a fixed mindset made up the inaccuracies.'

Indeed, in a ground-breaking study in the early 2000s (whose findings were published in a paper titled 'Unskilled and Unaware of It: How Difficulties in Recognizing One's

Own Incompetence Lead to Inflated Self-Assessments'), Cornell University students David Dunning and Justin Kruger demonstrated through research and experiments that unskilled employees who lack self-awareness often overstated their abilities and competence at their job.

And there are plenty of these people in organisational cultures. I've worked with a few myself, and probably even qualified as one early in my career.

Every cultural evolution program has to start with self-awareness. It must give people a window into who they are and what they're about, their personal strengths and their opportunities for improvement. After all, without an understanding of ourselves, it's hard for us to develop an understanding of others and be empathetic to their needs.

To be clear, I'm not talking about authenticity. Well, I am, but not in the way others talk about it. Authenticity is (according to my friends at Wikipedia) the degree to which one is true to one's own personality, spirit or character, despite external pressures.

Nice.

Researchers Erikson (1995) and Weigort (2009) found that it has more to do with a commitment to values and motivation and therefore is deeply personal and (crucially) 'incapable of challenge by others'.

And there's the rub.

Everyone's view of what is authentic is different and if I believe I'm authentic regardless of how I behave, well, that's just what I believe. There are no rules as to what it is. Since people's values, behaviours, motivation and communication styles differ, there can be no hard and fast rules.

There are misogynists, racists, and people who harass and bully others who believe themselves to be the most authentic people on the planet. Of course they're not, and I can say that because my view of authenticity is different.

Being told to 'be authentic' isn't altogether helpful; however, anyone can become the person they want to be through continual self-awareness and feedback. And often the latter will compel the former.

Some of the most self-aware people I know take the time to ask others for their opinions on their values, behaviours, motivations and communication style. They spend time thinking about what it is they stand for and whether that is in line with the way the world currently thinks and works.

These people never use age as an excuse; they don't put people into a box based on their gender, race or opinions; they stay on top of the skills they need to be good at what they do; and they strive to behave in a way that positively influences other humans around them.

They think before they speak, challenge rather than conform, listen when they want to talk, make time for learning *and* play, rest and recharge, and are productively busy with their time. They consistently practise at being the very best human being they can be, which requires resilience, courage and reflection.

This is the kind of authenticity we need to see, and we need people to share how they got there in a language and style that doesn't alienate or confuse.

What questions did they ask? What barriers existed and how did they remove them? How did their lifestyle change? And who are the people who helped them get there?

Although people's views of what authenticity means might differ, often the actions they need to take, and the behaviours they need to demonstrate to achieve a status where they can be a positive influence on others, are the same.

To become the best version of ourselves requires support, education, feedback, discipline and personal change. The culture should support all of these things.

Okay, where was I? Oh yes, self-awareness.

EMOTIONAL INTELLIGENCE

In 2013, researchers Zes and Landis found that 'Poor-performing companies' employees were 79 percent more likely to have low overall self-awareness than those at firms with robust ROR.' And that companies with a greater percentage of self-aware employees consistently outperformed those with a lower percentage.

So increased self-awareness produces tangible results. But wait, there's more.

Daniel Goleman determined that self-awareness was a critical component of emotional intelligence, which is a key contributor to cultural success. He found that 'what makes the difference between stars and others is not their intelligent IQ, but their emotional EQ'.

Readers who have worked in or seen great cultures know this to be true. The people we learn from, the people we spend most time around and the cultures we enjoy working in know how to behave, have discipline and focus, know how to get the job done in difficult circumstances and understand the value of continuous improvement. These are all traits of emotionally intelligent people, and when people like this work together the cultural results are the envy of others.

In his book *Emotional Capitalists: The New Leaders*, researcher and author Martyn Newman says,

> In the last 10 years, the most sensational strategy for achieving goals has been to focus on developing emotional intelligence. It is an indispensable set of

social and emotional competencies for leveraging knowledge and emotions to drive positive change and business success.

The importance of EQ in cultures has been downplayed for far too long. Quite how the hardest thing to develop and change has been classed as 'soft skills' is beyond me. Technical ability has taken precedence over how humans treat each other in cultures for most of my lifetime. Now the balance is finally shifting, and about time too.

High emotional intelligence has been proven to lift productivity, sales and overall team performance. This is why it is a core component of vibrant cultures.

Cultures that demonstrate low emotional intelligence (stagnant and combatant in the culture model in the figure on page 12 of this book) are almost always toxic, and nothing good is toxic.

The people within these cultures behave poorly and aren't aware they are the problem. Their actions include dissention, anger, gossip and silent resistance. They refuse to be part of the team or the solution that the team is looking to find. They are wedded to the 'way things are done around here' and will tell you 'it is what it is'. In an insightful blog in February 2019, the Chartered Institute of Personnel and Development's David D'Souza described how their thought-terminating clichés 'kill thought (and probably useful action)'.

From someone who doesn't want to do the job they were employed to do, to someone who shows disrespect for authority or their team/classmates, these low EQ people like to focus on their own agendas and obstruct progress. They believe in 'I' not 'we' and stand in the way of evolution.

If the research is to be believed, however, their days are numbered.

A 2018 *Harvard Business Review* article titled 'The Rise of AI Makes EQ More Important' reported that researchers had found, 'Skills like persuasion, social understanding and empathy are going to become differentiators as AI and machine learning take over other tasks.'

According to Dr Toby Walsh, Professor of Artificial Intelligence at Sydney University, machines will slowly take over jobs that are considered dull, dirty, difficult and dangerous. However, human beings who are high in emotional intelligence will always be required to lead other humans.

After the Global Financial Crisis the world changed, and the 'Greed is Good' mantra advocated by ruthless corporate raider Gordon Gecko in the movie *Wall Street* in the late 1980s is now called out—not championed—in media outlets and reports around the world. Sadly such greed still exists and many CEOs still place their personal interests far above those of their staff.

That said, emotional intelligence, with its focus on empathy, has never been more valued. It's a cultural investment that, with self-awareness, disciplined application and continual feedback, provides payback in almost every part of a culture. Indeed, achieving a vibrant culture as described in this book is only achievable with high EQ people.

The way most organisations *force* self-awareness in the hope of creating more emotionally intelligent staff is through the often-maligned personality survey.

TRAITS, EMPATHY AND STORIES

In the spirit of full disclosure here, let me say that I love a good personality survey. I love to read a report of who a set of algorithms thinks I am, based on spending 20 minutes answering questions that on the face of it look exactly the same. BUT, and it's a big 'but' (hence the caps), only if the language and the detail of the report observes three important criteria:

1. It uses language that I recognise and that encourages me to share my preferences. For example, it doesn't refer to me as an 'Intrepid Explorer' or an 'Adventurous Astronaut'. *Ugh*.

2. It doesn't purport to be exact and definitive. I'm a human being, and that means no manner of questioning, regardless of the research and the data behind it, can ever determine 100 per cent who I am and what I'm about. Some fallibility must be recognised.

3. It encourages the people with whom I've undertaken this exercise to share what we now know about our personality in order to increase empathy and allow us to change our communication style based on the person (or people) we're communicating with.

Almost all personality surveys in the marketplace today (and it's estimated that cultures spend over US$500 million every year on them in the US alone) are based on Carl Jung's extensive work on human personality and behaviour in the 1920s.

Personality traits are stable characteristics of individual differences that may be used to describe and to explain behaviour (cf. Hirschberg, 1978). They are the things we do consistently and without thinking.

What Jung found was that these traits are part of the human DNA and rely on how people gather information (sensing or intuition), how people make decisions (thinking or feeling) and how people react in social situations (introversion or extroversion).

Broadly, according to Jung, our personalities are made up of four elements, which, to make them more applicable to the way we work, I've paraphrased as *detail focus*, *people focus*, *action focus* and *social focus*.

No one is a 'pure' representative of one of these elements; most people have a measure of each element in their personality. Our predominant focus, however, is our main guide to how we see the world, make decisions and act in social situations.

Sigmund Freud's view on personality, however, was that it is made up of three (different) aspects that (like Jung's) together shape our behaviours. These are the *id* (the instinctual and emotional part of the mind concerned mainly with our needs and pleasures), the *ego* (which regulates these needs and pleasures with reference to reality) and the *superego* (our moral conscience).

There are many excellent blogs, books and tools that can help cultures to become more self-aware, to better interpret the personalities of their people and describe to others the way to interact with them.

When I undertook such an exercise with my team, my primary goals were always to improve empathy and communication skills, as the two go hand in hand.

Empathy is defined as the ability to understand or feel what another person is experiencing. 'In organisational awareness,' writes Chade-Meng Tan in his book *Search Inside Yourself*, 'you understand the feelings, needs and concerns of individual people and how those interact with those of others and the organisation as a whole.'

What he's saying, I believe, is that in cultures of self-aware individuals, you 'get' each other and adjust the way you interact with each other as a consequence. In the great working cultures I've been fortunate to be part of, this is absolutely the case. We'd create a safe environment and let people know in advance that the basis of great teams is understanding one another. We'd share some of ourselves, our interests, our communication preferences and the kind of environment we need to do our best work.

There is no way to be empathetic without asking questions and listening, yet listening is something that lots of people don't prioritise. According to researchers Janusik and Wolvin (2006), only 2 per cent of work time is spent listening, compared with 21 per cent of family time. So it's little wonder that people in our personal lives understand us better than those at work.

Reading these few lines on empathy won't make you empathetic, any more than reading a manual on car maintenance will make you a mechanic. It's something we must work on through personal change. It requires us to be a little vulnerable and to think before we speak—things we are typically not taught how to do.

Mirror neurons, found in the pre-frontal area of the brain, fire when we see someone else do something. Just this morning I was watching football (real football, the game the world plays) on the TV, and when a corner was swung into the penalty area I instinctively craned my neck to head the ball in! These are mirror neurons in action. Oh and naturally I took partial credit for the fact that Everton scored!

It has been argued (and the debate rages on in the scientific world) that mirror neurons enable us to feel the pain of others, that if you've experienced the pain yourself (of hitting your thumb with a hammer, say), then you are able to 'feel' what it's like when you see someone else do it. Supporters of this hypothesis have dubbed it the 'Empathy System'.

It's useful to know this, but more useful for people within the culture to take the time to sit, listen and talk to one another to better understand how they see the world.

Social events are a good way to do this, with one caveat: that they don't revolve around alcohol after work. This is a classic extrovert mistake. I know this because I made it many times early in my career. For events to be inclusive, they need to be devised by the culture and occur, where possible, within work hours.

At this point, you may be thinking, 'we're too busy to do that' or, my favourite, 'we're not allowed to do that', both of which are wrong. A culture should never be too busy to build relationships and despite being told by others that I couldn't do this (especially in government settings), we did it every month.

We even took a Tuesday afternoon off to paint each other's portrait! Now don't get me wrong, we hit every deadline we were set, the quality of our work was excellent and we ensured that a member of the team was contactable throughout. But eventually people stopped telling me that I couldn't do it and we had a list of people who wanted to join the team!

The last time I visited the Atlassian office in Sydney, one of the teams was playing bingo in the kitchen at 2 pm. No calls or deadlines were missed and no one was left out. It was a raucous event and a joy to behold.

Not only do people get to know each other better when they mix outside a work context, but they also create shared stories and experiences. And shared stories are a crucial part of any culture.

In his book *Homo Deus*, Yuval Noah Harari talks about the importance of stories to human culture. 'Meaning,' he suggests, 'is created when people weave together a common network of stories.' Gerry Johnson and Kevan Scholes identified stories as the number one element in their Cultural Web in 1992. These are the events and activities from the past that get talked about in and out of the office. Culture Amp (more about them later in the book), in their '6 Ways to Foster Belonging in the Workplace' study, found, 'Hearing frank and positive stories from all job levels can powerfully influence people's sense of belonging.'

There are many ways to build stories, but by building environments where positive ones can be created, cultures also enable greater empathy and thus facilitate more effective communication. And when it comes to communication, different people prefer different approaches.

As an extrovert, I'm more of a face-to-face person. I'm not a fan of email and if you're going to speak to me, you need to be positive and energetic. This is not the case for everyone. Some people prefer a calm approach that lists facts and data, for instance in email form or in a presentation. Some people like informal meetings in coffee shops; some people prefer formal meetings in designated meeting rooms.

Just as with listening, there's an assumption that everyone within a culture knows how to talk to one another and can moderate their approach accordingly, and this is not true. We learn how to communicate from our parents and the people we spend most time with.

Unless people within a culture are shown otherwise or work hard to learn from others, there will always be communication breakdowns, which will lead to a loss of engagement and may even mean that people aren't being the best versions of themselves in the office.

In their 2013 paper 'Introverts and Extroverts: Do Office Environments Support Both?', researchers Cushman and Wakefield proposed,

> If organisations want to change how teams/ departments with synergy collaborate, they must recognise the differing communication preferences in the workplace and provide an environment that meets employees' needs and also provides a support platform for collaboration.

Any shift in the culture requires staff to be given insights into how to change their approach depending on their audience.

This is something I do in the first half day of my culture programs and sets the tone for the rest of the time we spend together. Everyone has to do their bit for it to work.

I love this line from the Spotify Code of Conduct and Ethics: 'The vibe of our work environment is made up of how each and every one of us acts and speaks every day. So we are all responsible for it.'

IQ IS IMPORTANT TOO

Absent from this discussion so far is a word on IQ, so let me say here that being high in EQ alone isn't going to help a surgeon in an operating theatre, a baseball player to hit 40 home runs every year or a student to graduate, is it? Being a good human is important, but so too is knowing your stuff.

In his work Daniel Goleman describes IQ and technical skills as 'threshold capabilities' that are required to get a person into a job in the first place, but only with EQ can they go on to become a leader in their field.

Dr Carol Dweck also found that people with a growth mindset believe they can change with effort and set about doing just that.

When evolving a culture, an organisation must ensure its people have the necessary technical skills to complete the tasks they're asked to do and then use their emotional skills and judgement to apply them in the correct way in any given situation.

The cultures that succeed ensure that people are pushed forward, as we all do our best work on the edge of uncomfortable. This can only happen if they are both technically and emotionally good at what they do and have the judgement to know when to prioritise IQ over EQ or vice versa.

Problem solving may require greater application of IQ, while team building may require a greater application of EQ; it's simply not enough to have just one or the other. Organisations that ignore this run the risk of keeping brilliant jerks or nice idiots on the payroll. If that happens, there's only one place to look for the problem—the people who hire, develop and manage them.

All employees have to put in a shift and know their stuff, but without applying some basic human skills, they're always likely to hold the culture back.

CASE STUDY: Admiral Group

Admiral Group PLC are a financial services and insurance organisation based in the UK, with offices in Canada, France, Italy, India and Spain. They launched in 1993 with just one brand, no customers and 57 members of staff. Things have changed a bit since then!

One of their philosophies is 'that people who like what they do, do it better, so they ensure coming to work at Admiral is enjoyable'. To that end they encourage staff to create connections and to share how they're feeling.

In Italy there is a Ministry of Fun committee that organises events the entire organisation can participate in. Every month a different department within the business hosts an activity that brings people together, creates shared stories, increases empathy for the work others in the business have to do and, importantly, generates laughter! Events have included a Harry Potter Halloween month including Quidditch trials and snitch hunting!

KEY POINTS

- Self-aware people are the foundations for great culture.

- Empathy and communication skills can be learned.

- People have to know their subject matter and know to apply the balance of IQ and EQ that's most appropriate in a given context.

ACTION YOU CAN TAKE

Do a personality profiling exercise. I know. It seems like an obvious, somewhat hackneyed response to this section, but I'm almost certain you've been doing it wrong. If you run the exercise but focus on how to use the information to become more empathetic and to change your communication style, it changes everything (depending on your EQ of course).

Profiles that centre on the individual fail to pull down the barriers that currently exist and simply put people into boxes they may never climb out of.

PILLAR 2
VISION

At the heart of a great culture is an aspirational statement that ignites energy, motivation and passion. It describes where the culture seeks to be. This vision statement is a mantra that is referred to regularly by senior executives and that staff can then repeat without needing to refer to a piece of paper with it written on.

But before we get there, let's talk strategy.

ON THE EATING HABITS OF CULTURE

A business book on culture wouldn't be complete without outlining the eating habits of culture, as allegedly told by business guru Peter Drucker to Mark Fields, then President of Ford. But I'm not going to go there. I like what Daniel Ek, CEO of Spotify, has to say on it: 'There are people who say culture eats strategy for breakfast. That's bullshit. Great companies have both.'

And he's right (you can breathe a sigh of relief, Daniel). How can you have a great culture if you have no idea what it is you're trying to achieve? *And* if you haven't had breakfast? How is it possible to get the staff together and say, 'Let's co-create an experience that everyone wants to be part of!' without being able to answer the very obvious first question, 'Where are we going, again?'

In my 30 years of coalface experience two things always amazed me about how organisations—and their executive teams—approached strategy:

- the disproportionate time they spent developing it in relation to working on the culture to deliver it
- how quick they were to abandon it when the financial year started.

We used to write 10-year strategies, which may sound crazy in today's ever-changing landscape, but honestly it was crazy then too. They were almost always out of date within nine months and the six months spent on creating them was largely—and frustratingly quickly—rendered irrelevant. Today it's three years at the most.

But don't fall into the trap of trying to create the perfect strategy with no room for change. In Richard Branson's book *Like a Virgin: Secrets They Won't Teach You at Business School*, he cautions against trying to create perfection.

> There's an inherent danger in letting people think that they have perfected something. When they believe they've 'nailed it,' most people tend to sit back and rest on their laurels while countless others will be labouring furiously to better their work!

In my view, a good strategy should set a direct and achievable marker for the year(s) ahead. It should light a spark in people and set the organisation apart from those around it, regardless of the sector. It should be simple, straightforward, and grounded in honesty and reality. It's focused not on short-term fixes or unachievable projects, but on medium- to long-term investments with an element of risk that evolve the organisation into something better and more resilient than now.

It should be designed by the people who have to deliver it and should never be overdone. I've seen some organisations try to predict how much projects should cost and how long they'll take a year before they actually start planning, which is a recipe for disaster.

And everything should line up: goals and roles, hiring and firing, vendors and spenders ... okay, that's enough assonance for one day.

It should always answer the following questions:

- Why are we doing this?
- What do we want to achieve?
- How will we get there and how will we know?
- Who do we need to achieve it?

Strategies need to be multifaceted and cover items such as customer, data, technology, marketing and culture. The latter is often left off or else reduced to a paragraph written by HR at the last minute and full of words like *capacity*, *capability* and *resources*. It often provides a list of the latest training courses (that everyone else is doing) and policy changes, rather than activity that continually improves the culture to deliver the strategic intent.

Some organisations use the Cultural Web as a mechanism for developing a culture strategy. Written and released in 1992 by Gerry Johnson and Kevan Scholes, it has six factors:

1. stories
2. rituals and routines
3. symbols
4. organisational structure
5. control systems
6. power structures.

These factors can be used to provide organisational insights on what's working and what's not within the current culture. It can also provide a view of where the organisation would like to be, then an action plan can be created to fill the gaps.

Most cultures ask questions through engagement surveys. These regular insights are crucial to understanding what's *actually* going on within a culture so appropriate action can be taken. However, as Didier Elzinga, CEO of people and culture platform Culture Amp, said in an interview I conducted with him in March 2019, 'The engagement survey is just one input into whether the people strategy is working. The culture strategy comes first and the survey is part of that.'

It's simply not possible to build a perfect strategy, but it is possible to build an unrealistic one. Without realism, there's no passion. Without passion there's no action. And without action —well, you're screwed.

VISION

Let's assume that you've spent just enough time (and no more) building a strategy that is all of the positive things that I've just described. A full understanding of the culture required to deliver it now needs to be built, and that starts with a vision statement.

This vision statement expresses in a clear, transparent and unambiguous sentence where the culture wants to be in the short to medium term. Importantly, the vision should feel just a little out of reach. That is to say, it's achievable, but it will take sustained productive performance from committed people who live the values and demonstrate the behaviours (see 'Values' and 'Behaviour' pillars respectively) to get there.

If it's too grand, or not wholly within the control of the culture, then rather than feeling aspirational, it will act as a demotivator to those working within the culture, as they simply won't buy into it. A vision statement of 'Enabling the success of our people' will beat 'To be the best HR team in the world!' every single day.

Realism is critically important too. It's usually impossible for a department to go from dead last in sales to first within a year, so a better vision would be to set a goal to target an improved position within the tier. Once this has been achieved, the vision should be reset.

Once set, the vision statement should inform every decision, with employees continually asking themselves the following questions:

- Does the vision statement act as a motivator for staff and the subcultures they work within?

- Does the activity we undertake each day align with the vision?

- Does hiring this individual improve our chances of achieving the vision?

- Will this project provide the outcomes to improve our chances of achieving the vision?

- Is the vision still achievable?

If the answer to any of these questions is no, then activity should pause while its importance is assessed alongside other similar initiatives, or the vision statement should be revisited to ensure that it's fit for purpose.

A vision is definitely not a marketing statement, a long-winded call-to-arms or a string of buzzwords. It should never read like a Hallmark card.

It doesn't describe outcomes or responsibilities or talk about taking over the world. It's pragmatic, practical and personal, and should never need to be printed out or stuck up on a wall. Vision statements are lived, not laminated.

Researchers Rafferty and Griffin found in 2004 that 'in the absence of encouragement and confidence building efforts, articulating a vision may have a neutral or even negative influence on employees'. So it's important not to overcomplicate them.

Vision statements should be easy to remember—the fewer words the better. There are many examples of vision statements out there that are frankly just too long to ever stick in people's minds. Here are a few:

> Our vision is to use our size and scale to lead the change towards a circular and renewable fashion industry, all while being a fair and equal company. (H&M)

> One day, 30% of all retail transactions in the US will be online. People will buy from the company with the best service and the best selection. Zappos.com will be that online store. (Zappos)

> Harvard College will set the standard for residential liberal arts and sciences education in the twenty-first century. We are committed to creating and sustaining the conditions that enable all Harvard College students to experience an unparalleled educational journey that is intellectually, socially, and personally transformative. (Harvard College)

It's not that any of these vision statements are 'wrong'; after all, these are hugely successful organisations. It's just that their vision statements aren't that memorable, and as a result the aspiration is lost. They could just as easily say:

> World-leading renewable fashion

> To become the No. 1 online retail store

> Transforming the future for Harvard College students.

Here are some examples of vision statements I like:

A Just World Without Poverty
(Oxfam)

We Fulfil Dreams of Personal Freedom
(Harley-Davidson)

Inventing the Future of Play
(Lego)

Inspiring and Unifying New Zealanders
(New Zealand Rugby).

My favourite vision statement was that of the Walt Disney Company: 'Make People Happy'. It's short and easy to remember. It's aspirational, given the multiple interactions that their staff have with people all around the world, yet it's just a little out of reach because you can't please everyone!

I say it 'was' my favourite because they changed it a couple of years back. It's now this: 'To be one of the world's leading producers and providers of entertainment and information'. Again, it's not wrong, but which one resonates more with you?

Vision statements should exist at every level of an organisation, including projects, teams and departments. However, it's critical that they all harmonise, so staff can draw a straight line between the work they're doing each day and how it contributes to the success of the overall organisation. Otherwise, successful subculture results and performance won't necessarily link to those of the organisation. This connection must be logical so personal contribution is clear.

Or, as Rosamund Stone and Ben Zander say in their excellent book *The Art of Possibility*, 'A vision releases us from the weight and confusion of local problems and concerns, and allows us to see the long clear line.' It's also an important cultural evolution tool, providing a new statement of intent and generating the impetus to move away from the current status quo.

Cultures that don't regularly reset their vision statements (at least every one to three years) stagnate and prospective employees won't 'buy in' to what they're trying to achieve.

Refreshing the vision (and the culture) is especially important if the culture is moving towards more flexible or innovative ways of working. McKinsey identified this in its 2017 survey report *How to Create an Agile Organization*. Being clear on the vision is one of the three principles for a successful transition.

Similarly, consulting company Bain noted in a 2017 paper, 'Orchestrating Successful Digital Transformation', that digital initiatives not only need a vision of their own but need to ensure that 'everyone remains committed to it'. Carina Veksler and Doug VanDyke of Amazon Web Services backed this up in an interview in 2017 when they said, 'Digital transformation requires strong leadership to drive change, as well as a clear vision.'

An inspirational vision statement is also a great hiring tool. People are often attracted to cultures based on their aspirations, and it's a great way to check that potential employees share the same dreams and understand what it will take to get there.

This aspiration or purpose has never been more important for attracting new people. A Lovell Corporation survey of 2000 Gen-Zers (people born between 1995 and 2015) enthused, 'For the first time, we see a generation prioritizing purpose in their work.' Not that it wasn't there for other generations of course, and certainly in my experience the best people always ask what your future intentions are; it's just that this generation is *prioritising* it.

A vision statement is central to building and evolving a great culture, and when you have one it's essential that it's memorable and motivational.

One of the biggest mistakes organisations make with vision (and values and culture generally) is to bring in consultants or design agencies to work solely with their senior managers on crafting the necessary statements. This kind of activity sends a message to the rest of the staff that senior management own the definition of the culture and everyone else has to live it. An email is sent to everyone telling them what it is, often with some slick marketing materials, and they're encouraged to print it off as a reminder. When this happens, it makes it very easy for the staff to think or say, 'I haven't been involved in this, so it means nothing to me.'

Making this a senior-management-only activity is an old-fashioned quick-fix approach to culture in the same way that going open plan is with the working environment, and often the people involved in its creation do little to prove that it actually means anything to them. It then comes to be seen as an activity that the organisation undertook because they thought they should or because someone told them they should, rather than being a critical annual exercise that's required to continually refresh the aspirations of the culture and move it forward.

Cultures are the sum of everyone, not just senior management, therefore every subculture needs to be involved in the creation of the vision. It's a process I teach as part of my culture programs and takes 45 to 60 minutes to complete. Once you know how to do it, you never forget it. You also understand the importance of the vision and how to 'use' it every day.

MISSION

Some organisations forgo a vision statement and settle for a mission statement instead. Rather than being a statement of future aspiration, a mission statement articulates what the organisation exists to do for its customers and, often, for its staff. It essentially articulates its business strategy in a sentence or two.

When you read good mission statements you immediately get a sense of what an organisation does. Here are some good examples:

> To build the web's most convenient, secure, cost-effective payment solution
> (PayPal)

> To give customers the most compelling shopping experience possible
> (Nordstrom)

> Dedication to the highest quality of customer service, delivered with a sense of warmth, friendliness, individual pride and company spirit
> (Southwest Airlines)

> To accelerate the world's transition to sustainable energy
> (Tesla)

Facebook's mission statement—because I know you're itching to ask—is 'Give people the power to build community and bring the world closer together.' As a mission statement I think it's okay, because on the surface (easy there, cynics) that's what they are aiming to do. I would have said 'build safe communities' to ensure that data protection, ethics and basic human decency remain at the heart of what they do, but hey, I didn't get the gig, so it is what it is.

Some organisations have both a vision and a mission, which is absolutely fine provided that (a) they are distinctly different (i.e. aspirational and transactional) and (b) they make sense when you put them together. Here's a good example from IKEA: 'Our vision is to create a better everyday life for the many people. We make this possible by offering a wide range of well-designed, functional home-furnishing products at prices so low that as many people as possible will be able to afford them.'

In short, they're saying 'we want to improve your life and here's how we'll help with that'. Nice.

All this stuff can be a bit of a minefield, though. There are many vision statements masquerading as mission statements and vice versa. For example, JetBlue's mission is 'To inspire humanity'. To do that will take a lot more than maintaining reliable flight schedules and providing great service. Uber's is to 'ignite opportunity by setting the world in motion'. I like this as a vision statement, but it says nothing of the day-to-day activity, as PayPal's mission statement does.

I'm also wondering what happened to that bottle of water I used to get in the early days of Uber. But my therapist says I should let that go.

Whether or not you have a vision, mission or both, if you're to build a culture of accountability and transparency it's important that you have a statement of intent that's visible to staff and customers alike. And it's essential that the staff are heavily involved in its creation and that it's facilitated by someone who can add creativity and energy and ensure that people don't feel like it's 'been done to them'.

Once they've been written they need to be lived. Senior executives can't expect the rest of the culture to live the vision if they're not doing so themselves. And the culture needs to hold senior managers to account for not utilising the vision from day to day and week to week.

The vision should be the lifeblood of the organisation and constantly drive it forward. As Thich Nhat Hanh says in his book *The Art of Living*, 'Our dream gives us vitality. It gives our life meaning.'

CASE STUDY: the community

the community is an advertising agency in Miami, Florida. Formed in 2001, it set itself a vision of becoming one of the most progressive cross-cultural agencies operating at the intersection of culture, creativity and technology. It's a vision it has since achieved.

The organisation is deeply multicultural. More than 80 per cent of its workforce in the US belong to a multicultural or minority group. It has also built a commitment to working with women's support groups, LGBQT organisations and cultural centres.

For the past five years, it has been ranked as one of the top advertising agency innovators for talent growth and cultural diversity projects while it has expanded rapidly into digital and social media at a time when other agencies were simply watching. Its vision has fuelled everything it has done and has been used to consistently challenge not only its own way of doing things, but the industry in general.

The agency's President, Luis Montero, said in an interview, 'Growth is viewed solely in numbers. But we also see growth as the product of something bigger — following a vision.'

Its vision now extends out towards further transformation of the advertising agency business. Montero says it has looking to bring in 'coders, anthropologists, screenwriters, industrial designers, and artists. Great ideas can come from anywhere.'

KEY POINTS

- A vision is a statement of the future that feels just a little out of reach but still achievable.

- A mission is a statement of purpose and describes what an organisation does.

- A vision can be 'lived' only if employees have been involved in its creation. It's a collaborative exercise that unites employees for the future challenges ahead.

ACTION YOU CAN TAKE

Vision creation exercise (40 minutes)

1. In small groups, write on Post-it notes single aspirational words linked to the organisation's strategy. (5 minutes)

2. Create short sentences (3–6 words) from these Post-its using punctuation or linking words. (15 minutes)

3. Review each sentence to see if it can be written more eloquently or concisely. (10 minutes)

4. All vote on their preferred sentence. The most popular choice becomes the agreed vision statement. (10 minutes)

PILLAR 3
VALUES

If a vision is an aspirational statement of the future and the mission describes what the organisation does, then what are values?

I know, this stuff can get really confusing. So confusing in fact that lots of organisations bring in external people to create it on their behalf, and before you know it there's a brand refresh and the values are being hoisted front and centre to show how forward-thinking or woke the organisation is.

Blogs from seemingly legit sources scream 'Six values every culture should have!' or 'If you don't have these values you're irrelevant to millennials!'

But just because a culture has a set of 'values' or an organisation states publicly that it is 'values-driven' doesn't make it so. I may say I'm great at being a parent, and it might even be true, but if I'm just paying lip service to something that's really important, then sooner or later I'll get found out and my kids will divorce me. Which they may do when they read this. (Who am I kidding, they're never reading this!)

Some cultures make the mistake of using a values definition exercise to correct the behaviour of staff: 'Treat each other with respect!' Others get them mixed up with vision statements: 'Changing the way the world...'

Worse still are values that state the things that people should be doing by default. As Denise Lee Yohn stated in a *Harvard Business Review* article in February 2018, words such as collaboration, ethical, fun and customer-oriented should be inherent, so there should be no need to single them out as values that guide everything that a culture does.

In 2014, Maitland, a financial PR company, found that three words—integrity, respect and innovation—crop up continually in the values of FTSE100 companies in the UK.

Too many value definition exercises results in bland or beige, insincere statements that could be applied to just about any business in the world and don't actually reflect what the organisation—through its culture—is trying to achieve. Of course, it's easy to tell staff what the five values are following a senior management offsite, but if anything sets the wrong kind of tone for living the values, this exercise is it.

A select group of people in an expensive catered venue get to decide on behalf of everyone else what the guiding principles of the work they do should be. And if they get them wrong they can backfire spectacularly.

Volkswagen are a very recent case study of values failure. Their decades-long falsification of emission results led to the resignation of CEO Martin Winterkorn and a worldwide investigation into its practices.

In the company's 2015 annual report, Chairman Hans Dieter Potsch said, 'The misconduct uncovered in fiscal year 2015 runs contrary to all of the values that Volkswagen stands for.' Those values, as listed in the 2014 annual report were:

- customer focus
- top performance
- creating value
- renewability
- respect

- responsibility

- sustainability.

Almost overnight in 2015 it became clear to customers and shareholders that these values were compromised by certain individuals and ultimately the management team, leading to resignations and a restructure.

That's the thing with values. Unless they're practised consistently at every level of the organisation, they become mere words in an annual report, or on a poster or webpage, that matter little to those who work in the culture.

Potsch said at a press conference in Germany that there had been a 'chain of errors', not just a 'one off' and that the culture was one that tolerated rule breaking.

THE VALUE OF VALUES

In his book *First Things First*, Stephen Covey identifies values definition as a 'Compass' activity—that is to say, it is an important mechanism in setting the emotional direction. Values are statements of what the culture holds to be true and how people will work together. They have to be specific to what the organisation and its culture believes and, critically, to be used to hire people who believe the same things.

This is the true value of values. Not only do you build a culture full of people who want the same things, you create a desire from others outside the culture who also believe those things. This is why great cultures continue to attract great people. Those individuals aren't just good at what they do technically; they also have a belief system that matches those of the culture that they want to join.

Often when there is a change in management the culture can be affected either positively or negatively depending on whether the new people hold the values in the same regard as the previous ones did.

They are also a statement—when they are upheld every day—to investors, shareholders, stakeholders and customers that the organisation, through its culture, knows how to keep its promises.

Facebook cop a lot of flak—rightly in my opinion—for their position on privacy. Yet collecting and sharing information in order to connect people and products is something that Facebook value.

Indeed they have a value specifically for that—it's called 'Build Social Value'. They are simply being true to their values, whether people like it or not.

Mike Cannon-Brookes, co-founder of Atlassian, said it best. He talked about the fact that when they're hiring they accept that people's skills and their jobs may change, but the 'fundamental base attributes of how those people treat the world, treat other people and treat their customers won't change over the lifetime of the company.'

SAY WHAT YOU MEAN

Having spent time at Atlassian and talking to their staff, I can say with confidence that they live their values out in the open. They perfectly represent what I've observed both inside and outside the office. And while I'm sure like most cultures there are occasions when people don't apply them (because you cannot manufacture a perfect individual or culture), they are committed to ensuring that the culture continually evolves behind these five values:

1. Open company, no bullshit.

2. Build with heart and balance.

3. Don't #@!% the customer.

4. Play as a team.

5. Be the change you seek.

It's immediately obvious when you read these that the way these values have been written can be confronting, and if you don't like this, then that's a sure sign that Atlassian is not an organisation you want to work for, because you don't value things in the same way they do.

That's why it's important to write values in a way that represents what the organisation truly stands for—not glib, generic marketing statements, but things you can stand behind and explain in the context of the customers you serve.

Having worked in government for eight years I can categorically say that a value of 'Don't #@!% the customer' wouldn't be appropriate, although I feel like I'm missing out on an opportunity to take a pop at politicians. Another time…

'Do good for the public' might be a more appropriate way of saying something similar.

For the values statements to become part of the fabric of the way you work, they have to mean something within that context. They cannot be abstract or decoupled from what the organisation exists to do. Or, as author Patrick Lencioni put it, 'Cookie-cutter values don't set a company apart from competitors; they make it fade into the crowd.'

This is why you can't copy the values of another culture. It's also why your culture has to be involved in their creation.

Culture Amp is a people and culture platform that captures feedback from employees that cultures can then use to tailor programs to improve the experience they provide for their employees. Like Atlassian, their values perfectly represent what they're about. Founder and CEO Didier Elzinga said this: 'Values are not created, they're uncovered. Like carving a bear from a block of stone, you aren't creating it, you're uncovering it by removing everything that's not the bear.'

Culture Amp's values are:

- Have the courage to be vulnerable.
- Learn faster through feedback.
- Trust others to make decisions.
- Amplify others.

They have an excellent series of blogs on how they uncovered their values and offer up some great tips to help others do likewise.

Zappos is an online shoe retailer based in Las Vegas. Their CEO Tony Hsieh fully admits he knows nothing about shoes, but he knows how to do culture well. He says that one of the keys to their continued success is the values they have at the heart of their culture. In his book, *Delivering Happiness: Profits, Passion and Purpose*, he writes, 'You gotta love the game. To become really good you've got to live it and sleep it.'

Zappos have 10 core values:

1. Deliver WOW through service.
2. Embrace and drive change.
3. Create fun and a little weirdness.
4. Be adventurous, creative and open-minded.
5. Pursue growth and learning.
6. Build open and honest relationships with communication.
7. Build a positive team and family spirit.
8. Do more with less.
9. Be passionate and determined.
10. Be humble.

They summarise their culture in a book that they make public, and they run a culture camp for others keen to gain insights into how they've set the organisation and its staff up for success.

HOW DOES A 'VALUES-DRIVEN' ORGANISATION ACT?

That's another thing that's great about organisations like Zappos, Atlassian and Culture Amp: they give away everything about what makes them tick. Playbooks, blogs, videos, camps—it's all there for you to read, watch, download and experience, then you can decide how to do it yourself. They want their customers and anyone who happens to stumble onto their website to be successful at great culture too.

This is the kind of thing a values-driven company does. They don't say, 'Look how successful we are', then keep it to themselves. They live their values inside and out and use them to make priority calls and acquisitions, and to hire people to help them continue their perpetual cultural journey.

They don't just talk about them; they actively bring them to life in everything that they do, including the way they hire and welcome new people into the culture.

A lot has been written and talked about with regard to hiring for cultural fit, and of course most organisations can't do it because they haven't taken the time to define their culture, so there's nothing to hire against. Instead, a standard set of questions, technical skills, qualifications and psychometric testing fill the gaps.

Where time, money and effort have been invested to define the culture, it's imperative that it's used to bring in the kind of people who will continue to add to it rather than hold it back.

The hiring process is not an exercise in finding someone with a pulse to fill a gap to complete a ridiculous program of work that wasn't achievable from day one. It's an opportunity to bring in an individual whose values, intention, mindset and ambition match those of the organisation.

While their skills may get their foot in the door, it's their values and emotional intelligence that will win them the job, and the interview should be structured to ensure that these are the things you uncover.

It may take one, two or seven interviews to do that, however; to ensure that a force for good is added to the culture, time needs to be taken to do this exercise well. That way the person fully understands what is expected of them and the environment in which the work is done, so time isn't wasted on unnecessary performance management.

Questions should be tailored to the values of the individual and how they demonstrate these day to day. This includes questions around how they would apply them and remain resilient in stressful situations.

As social satirist and former host of *The Today Show* Jon Stewart once said, 'If you don't stick to your values when they're being tested, they aren't values, they're hobbies.'

The aim of the interviewing process is to separate those who understand what the values stand for and how to practise them, from those who just want a job and will tell the interviewer what they think they want to hear.

If organisations such as Zappos hired people who didn't share their values, their culture would become stagnant very quickly as these people would 'drag' others down with them.

This is why Zappos have a very well defined recruitment and induction process, which they call 'The Zappos Family New Hire Program'. Every single new hire goes through the four-week program, regardless of their role or the department they have joined. According to the Zappos website, it is 'a combination of technical training and culture immersion'.

Values, customer service, technical tools and on-the-job training. Indeed after two weeks, all new hires hit the phones and start taking incoming calls from customers. There's also an opportunity to build relationships with other employees through a series of welcoming sessions. And at the end of all that is a celebration of what they've achieved—and away they go!

Of course, Zappos' culture is not for everyone and at the end of the four weeks it may be determined that rather than continue working in an environment where their values don't match, they can take a financial payout not to join. For most cultures, that may seem like a ridiculous idea, yet when you take into consideration the potential cultural degradation, reputation loss and use of management time to performance manage people who don't want to be there, it makes perfect sense.

When I tell this story during my keynotes and programs, the main thing I hear is 'We couldn't do that in our culture!' and for most that is the reality. Which is what probation periods are used for. If at the end of the probation, the person doesn't display the values expected of them or meet the expectations that were set, it's time to say goodbye, for all the reasons laid out in the previous paragraph.

It's just that most people use the probation period as a rubber-stamping exercise, rather than a values fit assessment.

The same can be said of the corporate induction program. On my first day in one of my roles my new boss was at another office (she called the next day) and I was directed to read the intranet and given a copy of the acronym dictionary!

There were no introductions to staff, equipment ready to go or culture deck to familiarise myself with. To say I was underwhelmed was an understatement. In fact, by handing me the acronym dictionary the organisation was saying,

'Here's how complicated we've made things and we expect you to uphold this.'

On the positive side, part of my role was to address the team culture and I had a couple of things to go on straight away.

I'm always astounded by the disparity between the time and care taken to interview and prepare an offer and the lack of care given to welcoming someone into the team.

Like Zappos', Atlassian's 90-day induction is an experience in itself. Two days ('Rocket Fuel') to get people acquainted with the basics followed by a 30-day, well-defined education and familiarisation program. For the second 30 days 'suggestions' are made about things new people could explore, while for the final 30 days staff are encouraged to build their own adventure.

By day 91 they should feel like they are 'in residence'.

Pinterest sends their new hires an introductory email containing their induction schedule and they are provided with an opportunity to introduce themselves to the company before actually starting. Then, as with Zappos, all new hires start the induction process together with breakfast on the first day.

At Twitter, that first-day breakfast is with the CEO!

Whatever you decide to do, make sure you welcome people in a way that makes them feel valued immediately, as there's nothing worse than a culture that talks about people being its most important asset and then actively demonstrates that this is not the case.

When done well, values can be an incredible asset to an organisation, but it's important that they're not used as a weapon. Identifying and defining them is an important exercise, and staying true to them requires courage and determination.

CASE STUDY: Elite SEM

Founded in 2004, Elite SEM is a US-based digital marketing agency that specialises in services such as search engine optimisation (SEO) and paid social media. In January 2019 it was voted the #1 place to work in marketing and media in the *Ad Age* awards.

When founder Ben Kirshner created the agency he believed the advertising agency model was broken. In an interview he said, 'Sales people...were getting paid a lot of money and weren't doing much work. The account managers were getting paid very little and then they would just leave.' He saw that their staff turnover averaged around 20 to 30 per cent. So he set about creating a different model, one that shares fee percentages with account managers, thus creating a meritocracy where customer success leads to staff success.

Their four core values are:

1. Love what you do
2. Circle of education
3. Attitude of gratitude
4. Strive for greatness.

Kirshner is extremely proud of Elite SEM's low staff turnover rate, which he attributes partly to the hiring process, insisting they are 'very, very particular' about who they bring into their culture.

In an interview in *Inc.* magazine, he said, 'Our interviews are really based on core values.' Using *Attitude of Gratitude* as an example, he explained, 'The hiring team will ask candidates a lot of questions to gauge how grateful a candidate is; how much they appreciate others and how much they give back.' This includes asking when they last did a good deed for someone — bought them coffee or lunch, say. If they're not able to demonstrate that they exhibit this value, then they don't make it through.

In a separate interview, CEO Zach Morrison said, 'Everyone is involved in creating, maintaining, and evolving our culture. It's then leadership's responsibility to steward that culture and make sure it aligns with the company's values.'

And if you haven't hired for those values in the first place, then evolving the culture will become extremely difficult.

KEY POINTS

- Values must be lived and this will require courage.
- Values must be specific to the organisation, not bland and generic.
- Values should be used in the hiring process.

ACTION YOU CAN TAKE

When determining the values of your culture, representatives from all areas of the culture (including but not limited to senior management) should be involved. You should start by talking about what makes the organisation different from its competitors or those that do similar work. Larger groups should be split into smaller groups.

Key words should then be captured on cards and conversations encouraged about how these words would be 'lived' on a day-to-day basis. The urge to simply write values down straightaway should be avoided, as it's the discussion that will bring clarity to the things the culture stands for.

Once the teams have spent time discussing these words and how they would be lived, then time should be provided for each group to craft their value statements. Provide examples of other (similar) organisations so the tone is understood, but the intention here is not to copy anyone else.

The aim for each group of people is to create four value statements. Once this has been done, they are put to a democratic, binding vote. Once the four have been agreed on, it's important to then come up with a list of how they will be demonstrated day to day. You can have some fun with this exercise by getting people to act them out or else produce videos that talk about what it means to demonstrate them.

End the exercise with a small celebration with the CEO (or similar) expressing gratitude for the important work that's been done.

PILLAR 4
BEHAVIOUR

If you knew your behaviour at work was going to be discussed publicly, would you still act in the same way? What about if your family could see a video of your daily interactions with others at work? Would that make you think differently about how to treat those around you? Would you be proud of your own behaviour?

These are important questions, and I want to make this point absolutely clear. What holds an organisation back from meaningful and lasting cultural change isn't technology, working environments, process or a lack of innovation time. It is almost always the mindset and behaviours of its people.

This fact has been ignored for far too long.

Organisations and individuals have always found ways to explain this away. By highlighting small increments in remuneration or investments in new technology. By making grand statements about how they'll stay in touch with the future. Or by reminding staff and the public of statements that senior managers made to the press, only to act quite differently back at the office.

It is behaviour, not goals or objectives, that sets the benchmark for continual change and sustained performance, so it's only right that this is the first of the critical pillars for cultural evolution.

Back when I started work in 1987 I was told it was more important to be respected than to be liked. This advice was routinely dispensed to those my age making their first foray into the working environment. The inference was that you deliver on what needs to be done, sometimes in spite of rather than in collaboration with the people around you. That you treat people how you feel you need to in order to get results, no matter how it may make them feel.

I remember feeling conflicted by this advice. I'd spent my school days avoiding fights and bullies and trying to fit into a world I didn't really feel a part of. I made up stories, made people laugh and looked forward to the day when I could earn money to gain some level of independence.

I had no idea what that entailed, but I felt sure that it couldn't be any worse than what I was leaving behind. Yet, when I finally did join the workforce I found that most of the issues I'd seen at school still existed in work, driven by people who were old enough to know better. Bullying, sexism, poor performance, disruptive influences and unethical behaviour were rife.

I'd like to say that I only saw this in the 1980s, but that wouldn't be true. I saw it in the 1990s, 2000s and 2010s. Indeed, in one of my later roles I was told that if I wanted to be in the C-suite — I didn't — then I'd have to be better at playing the political game, which is senior management speak for lying, cheating and playing people off against each other for personal gain. How many politicians do you know who behave honourably all the time? Exactly. That's the political game for you.

Yet, when I think back to my early days in work and throughout my career, a small handful of people have had a huge impact not just on the path I chose, but also on the person I have become. What they all had in common was that they knew their stuff, they had discipline, and they knew how to treat other people with empathy and respect.

In short, they were emotionally intelligent humans who knew how to behave well.

BEHAVIOURS DEFINE A CULTURE

If you want to change your culture, then some of the people (possibly including you) are going to have to change their behaviours and, make no mistake, this is likely to be the hardest thing they'll ever have to do, because some of these habits are hard to break.

If you're wondering how you're going to do that with a team or class full of people, then remember that it always *starts with you*. You have to show others how to do it consistently well and never fall back to the old ways of behaving.

You can't simply tell someone to change. You have to inspire them and then hold them to account.

Some people won't want to do it. They'll blame their upbringing, their age, other team members, their lack of knowledge, technology or the weather—trust me, there'll be something. George Bernard Shaw said,

> People are always blaming their circumstances for what they are. I don't believe in circumstances. The people who get on in this world are the people who get up and look for the circumstances they want, and if they can't find them, make them.

Key to changing behaviour is knowing how to control one's behaviour. As I discussed under 'Personality & communication', emotionally intelligent people are able to read the signs and adapt their behaviour accordingly. They can do this because their brain is sending them messages that they're able to interpret and act upon. And the brain likes to press our buttons.

The pre-frontal cortex (PFC) is the part of the brain that deals with the bad stuff. The PFC (which, for Monty Python fans, has nothing to do with the PFJ) makes decisions then generates rash or unwarranted behaviour. It's where humans process anger, fear and aggression. So if you're looking for a scapegoat for appalling behaviour start with the PFC, but remember that self-aware people are always in control of their physical reactions.

Too many cultures have been brought down by the behaviours of people who didn't read the signs and chose to react in a way that was destructive. Not only to the cultures in which they worked, but also in the industry—in the case of Enron, the financial markets.

The role of leaders is to create more leaders. We need more growth mindset role models who consistently demonstrate the required behaviours, so people within the culture have someone to follow.

Such leaders value the opinions of others, and listen and communicate effectively with others. They provide regular feedback, coaching and mentoring, and always have time for other people. They are disciplined, have good balance in their lives and look for ways to constantly evolve who they are in order to meet the changing nature of today's world.

In 2000 researchers Burton and O'Reilly reported, 'Behavioural theories concentrate on what a leader does rather than who a person is. However, studies show that followers tend to look first at who a leader is.' Unfortunately senior managers in organisations often don't recognise this, and then wonder why poor behaviour and performance are rife within their 'toxic' culture.

Many organisations today are investing in digital transformation programs, but too often the emphasis is on the digital element and they are discovering that simply implementing new technology does not of itself bring about transformation. This occurs only when the behaviours of those using it change.

In a paper in 2017 consulting company Bain concluded, 'The true digital leaders pull away from the competition by linking a bold strategic ambition to the...capabilities and behaviours that they will need to achieve it.' They listed their top three success factors as:

1. alignment at the top

2. agreement on priorities

3. change in corporate behaviours.

You need the first two to launch the initiatives and the third to achieve the outcomes from them.

McKinsey concurred, suggesting, 'Winners [in digital reinvention] are less likely to be hindered by soiled mindsets and behaviour.' And again, in a different paper later that year, 'implementation requires senior managers to role model the behaviours they expect of others'.

Leadership is not a development program or something that comes with a position within a hierarchy. It is a series of choices an individual makes that sets them apart from what they see around them. They stand up for those who don't have a voice and go to battle where ill-discipline, poor ethics and inhumanity reign.

To be this kind of person and to create a positive impact, all of the people within a culture need to examine themselves. They need to challenge the assumptions they have about themselves and others, to challenge their biases and predilections. They need to analyse every action they take—personal and impersonal—and ask themselves whether it enhances the wellbeing of others. They need to resist negative thoughts and ideas, to look inward (and often outward) for guidance on the correct action to take. By demonstrating these kinds of behaviours, leaders can change the attitudes of others within a short space of time.

The theory of cognitive dissonance was developed by social psychologist Leon Festinger in the 1950s. He and his team were able to prove that direct experience of positive behaviour leads to attitudinal change in people working within a culture.

He found that even if the behaviours being demonstrated were unfamiliar, people's need for consistency incrementally affected the way they felt and thought. By consistency he meant those small things that are demonstrated again and again that reinforce the individual's values and that lead to personal and operational improvement.

In short, good behaviour is infectious: if we see others doing it, we're more likely to do it ourselves. In his book *Gut Feelings: The Intelligence of the Unconscious*, Gerd Gigerenzer argues that personal behaviours rely on three things:

1. *Self-awareness*—how well you know yourself and are able to interpret and control your actions

2. *Rules*—the values and principles of the culture you work within

3. *Social environment*—how others around you act and behave.

PEOPLE BECOME WHO THEY SURROUND THEMSELVES WITH

This last point is important, because the behaviour of the people we choose to surround ourselves with within the culture directly impacts who we become.

As American leadership author Jim Rohn famously expressed it, 'You're the average of the five people you spend the most time with'. Twitter user @debihope put it slightly more directly in 2010: 'Before you diagnose yourself with depression and low self-esteem, first make sure you are not, in fact, surrounding yourselves with assholes'.

One of the biggest problems that cultures create for themselves is in not agreeing on the behaviours required of each other. There's a tendency to think that everyone should understand what's required and that the code of conduct is there to pick up those who don't.

In reality, however, it doesn't work that way and too often the onus is put on individuals to prove that a person behaved badly in a particular way, at which point they're either told by the HR department that 'it's too hard' to do anything about it, or it gets buried in the hope that everyone will forget about it. Which is what happened at Google in 2016 when one of its most senior executives was forced to resign over allegations of sexual assault, yet was still paid an exit package of US$35 million.

It would have taken a huge amount of courage for the complainant to step forward, and to have her complaint handled in this way would have been devastating. Worse still was that they chose to bury that information rather than making it public. It surfaced two years later only when shareholders took Google's parent company Alphabet to court.

It takes courage not only to change one's behaviour, but also to challenge those whose conduct fails to meet the agreed standards. Agreeing on these standards is a relatively straightforward process by comparison. They will differ from team to team. For example, the code of conduct required by a call centre team will be different from what is required by the engineering team. If the subculture is to achieve its goals, it's important that it has the autonomy to set these standards rather than having enterprise-wide behaviours imposed upon it.

It's a matter of identifying the behaviours you would like to see become consistent practices and of instilling the discipline of actually doing them and holding each other to account. The latter was identified by Patrick Lencioni as a particular problem. In his excellent book *The Five Dysfunctions of a Team*, he identified 'the need to avoid personal discomfort prevents team members from holding each other accountable for their behaviours and performance' as dysfunction number four.

He's putting cultures on notice here, implying that if you don't experience discomfort through behaviour change then you're doing it wrong, or as Dan Pink puts it in his book *Drive*, 'Becoming ever better at something you care about is not lined with daisies and spanned by a rainbow.' If only!

When the team has agreed on the behaviours, then it becomes easy to break them down into daily actionable things and to hold each other to them. When displayed they should be applauded and celebrated, as changing the habits created around behaviour requires continual support.

Once the culture starts to display the behaviours with regularity, then everything (and I do mean everything) becomes easier, and subcultures set the example for others in the organisation to follow. There's more laughter, greater productivity, improved relationships, better decisions and increased all-round engagement.

I love this line from Daniel Coyle's book *The Culture Code*: 'We tend to think group performance depends on measurable abilities like intelligence, skill, and experience, not on a subtle pattern of small behaviours. Yet those small behaviours [make] all the difference.'

SECRETS AND LIES

At one organisation I worked for we decided to restructure to meet a revised operational budget target. These kinds of exercises are extremely difficult as you're affecting the livelihood of the people doing their best to help the team to achieve its goals. But if you want to be a manager, that's what you are paid to do.

In true Morocco Mole style, we chose not to tell anyone. This was only the second restructure I'd been involved in as a senior executive, and with the other one (at a different company) we'd made it public. So in my defence—although as I write this it definitely feels like an excuse — I didn't really know what was considered 'normal'.

About three weeks after we'd started talking about it, however, I found out which was the right way to do things when one of my team asked me about the project we were working on. I was gobsmacked! I asked him how he knew what was going on, and he told me someone in HR had told him.

Cue some furious back-pedalling from the executive team, leading to high-level communications about the activity we were undertaking. By this time, pretty much everyone in the department knew about it and trust in our leadership ability had been eroded. Because secrets are bad for culture. They cause anxiety and stress, and are bad for morale and productivity, whether or not people find out about them at the time. They send the message that only this elite group can be trusted with this information.

Often the release of bad news is deliberately timed to minimise its impact. Attempting to 'bury' bad news can be as damaging as keeping it secret. There have been many high-profile examples of this scam.

Computing company Commodore declared bankruptcy after hours on Friday, 29 April 1994. Even its most senior executives were kept in the dark, only learning of the collapse via the news or the press release pinned to the office door.

On 11 September 2001, while the world was watching the tragedy unfold at World Trade Plaza in New York, Jo Moore, who worked as an adviser and press officer to the Chief Secretary of the UK Government's Transport, Local Government and the Regions, Stephen Byers, sent an email saying, 'It's now a very good day to get out anything we want to bury. Councillors expenses?' The email was leaked to the press and Moore was swiftly sacked.

Still in the UK, back in December 2006, Tony Blair became the first sitting Prime Minister to be interviewed by police as part of a criminal inquiry. He was widely criticised for choosing to do so on the day the report into Princess Diana's death was released.

Whatever the news, it should always be delivered openly, honestly and quickly. This is something that those in the medical profession and emergency services are taught as part of their induction into public service. In a paper for the *Western Journal of Medicine* titled 'Communicating bad news', Miranda and Brody state, 'The physician's goal…is to fully inform the patient and family so that they are able to comprehend the clinical situation and make sound decisions consistent with their beliefs and ideals.'

It's no different in the business world. In order to preserve the culture of the organisation and the trust of its employees (the general public and shareholders), senior managers have a responsibility to be honest about their position and to outline the work required to ensure the goodwill within the culture is maintained.

Sugar-coating the news, obscuring the activity behind an abstract name ('project refocus') or being economical with the truth only creates fear and distrust.

This is something that former Netflix executive Patty McCord talks about in her book *Powerful: Building a Culture of Freedom and Responsibility*.

> We didn't want anyone, at any level, keeping vital insights and concerns to themselves. The executive team modelled this: We made ourselves accessible, and we encouraged questions. We engaged in open, intense debate and made sure all of our managers knew we wanted them to do the same.

Jason Fried and David Hannemeir Hansson, in their book *ReWork*, observe, 'People will respect you more if you are open, honest, public and responsive during a crisis. Don't hide behind spin or try to keep your bad news on a down low.'

Cultures whose leaders limit bad news to a few people and who encourage a culture of selective confidentiality are not to be trusted. They have made the decision to behave in a way that is disrespectful. Once the news becomes common knowledge, the leaders' previous efforts to suppress it will erode confidence in their ability to lead the organisation to a more successful future.

Conversely, organisations that communicate early, that are honest about their position and what it might mean, that take the time to clearly articulate the process and involve others in it, and that treat staff with empathy and understanding increase engagement, trust and confidence.

Any kind of news that negatively affects the culture is never easy to deliver, but senior managers can make it a lot easier to bear and protect what currently exists if they're honest and open from the start.

CASE STUDY: ING, Zappos

Dutch bank ING offer a rare case study of exemplary practice when it comes to challenging poor behaviours to achieve cultural evolution. When moving to a different and more flexible way of doing things, they recognised that behaviour and the mindsets associated with it had to change.

Former Chief Operating Officer Bart Schlatmann declared in 2015, 'We have spent an enormous amount of energy and leadership time role modelling the sort of behaviour — ownership, empowerment, customer centricity — that is appropriate for a [new] culture.' They started their evolution program with self-awareness and personality testing, followed by a period when senior management role modelled what good behaviour looked like so others could follow suit.

Not everyone within the culture wanted to embrace the new behaviours, and this inevitably led to redundancies. Schlatmann said, 'We lost a lot of people who had the right knowledge, but not the right mindset.'

There is always a fear that losing people will adversely affect performance. In my experience, however, losing those with poor behaviours almost invariably has a positive impact.

Zappos' CEO Tony Hsieh, in his book *Delivering Happiness: Profits, Passion and Purpose*, recalls how after a round of redundancies in 2000,

> We realized that we had laid off the underperformers and the nonbelievers, but because everyone remaining was so passionate about the company and believed in what we were doing, we could still accomplish just as much work as we had before.

KEY POINTS

- Behaviour change is crucial for any kind of transformation.

- Knowledge of behaviour change is one thing, action and accountability quite another.

- Keeping secrets is bad for culture, even if no one knows!

ACTION YOU CAN TAKE

In teams, create a list of good behaviours (I have a deck of 21 cards). Go through each and what they mean in reality. Pick the five behaviours that you and the team want to work on. Come up with five examples of how they would be demonstrated on a practical level day to day.

Each person should pick at least one of the five to work on. Set up a regular meeting to hold each other to account for the promises you've made to each other. Where progress hasn't been made, the culture needs to reinforce the importance of behaviour and why action always speaks louder than words.

RECOGNITION & REWARD

I've just finished watching the highlights of this year's Oscars ceremony, where once a year those involved in the making of movies come together to celebrate the success of the industry and to reward those deemed to have performed best in their roles.

Reward and recognition are very much the exception to the rule in the world of work, yet celebrating and rewarding the little moments is what keeps cultures fresh and evolving.

Demonstrating values or a behaviour change, achieving a milestone or marking a birthday—there are no big trophies or gushing speeches on these occasions, just an acknowledgement of the efforts involved to achieve the goal. Even if, it's not dying for a year.

Vibrant cultures recognise that in order to keep moving forward, recognising and rewarding the efforts of their people is an important motivator and serves to inspire others. It is these small moments, when people take a break from their day-to-day routine, that help people to take stock of where they are, where they've come from and what's required — mindset and effort — to achieve the next set of goals.

When I start working with a new client, I often find that this part is missing. Priority and time aren't given to celebrating the small things, although there may be financial incentives via an outdated appraisal system at the end of the year.

Where money is the main motivator, people are often suspicious. With the lack of transparency, animosity lurks just beneath the surface. That's not to say that remuneration is not important to a culture — it's fundamental in attracting and retaining people — but only those who demonstrate the values of the organisation and smash through the work offer a role model for others.

Pay and conditions must be as transparent, fair and equitable as possible. Paying people more or less depending on their sex, race or national base is an abhorrent practice that many cultures still need to address.

As I write this, it's playing out in the US where the national women's soccer team have taken legal action against their own governing body, the US Soccer Federation (USSF). They assert that they carry out the same responsibilities — personally and as a team — to promote the game as their male counterparts, but have consistently been paid less. This is despite the fact that the US team is the most successful in the history of women's soccer! What's more, it has had far more on-field success, earned more profit and had larger TV audiences than the men's team.

This is just one, high-profile example of the work still to be done around gender equity, and while the contributions made by women are celebrated through initiatives such as International Women's Day, there is still not enough tangible action around some of the basic day-to-day issues (pay being one) to ensure parity for all.

In the example of the USSF, the court papers submitted in March 2019 state that the USSF claim that 'market realities are such that women don't deserve to be paid equally to the men'.

At an event to advocate for the Paycheck Fairness Act at the Capitol in Washington DC in January 2019, US Congresswoman Alexandria Ocasio-Cortez stated, 'We implicitly recognise, as women, that the pay gap and the wage gap is an injustice that persists through secrecy and it's an injustice that persists to the present day.'

Every culture needs to give equal recognition to the efforts of all and to address inequality and injustice as a priority. Whether it's female or minority employees, in developed or developing countries, every person should be paid fairly and equally for the work they do.

It should also set unambiguous goals to ensure that everyone understands the contribution they personally have to make to help evolve the culture.

WHAT ARE THE GOALS?

Cultures work best when the things they are collectively looking to achieve, and the behaviours expected while doing so, are clear and there is no room for misinterpretation. There's no surer way to kill motivation than to set goals that are unachievable or that leave room for individuals to decide for themselves what they think is needed.

Goals come in all shapes and sizes and are identified by a myriad different names, which are often used inter-changeably, including benefits, outcomes, key performance indicators (KPIs), targets, metrics, objectives, result areas and measures.

Whatever route you decide to take, remember that cultures work best when goals are easy to understand, involve stretch performance and are made public. Secrecy breeds distrust, fear and suspicion. Motivational speaker Tony Robbins said, 'Setting goals is the first step in turning the invisible into the visible.' I like this. And yet almost every culture I've worked in has had a process of setting goals at an organisational level then *cascading* (yep, they use this word) down to an individual level, usually behind closed doors. The achievement of these goals led to personal reward, often financial, at the end of the year.

Cascading anything is a relic of the command and control era and relies on those 'above' achieving their goals or at least taking action so those 'below' can do likewise and everyone can achieve their objectives. Result!

In my experience, this approach led to selfishness, and the team often suffered. When we took the initiative and openly shared our goals and looked to combine them at a team level, it dramatically changed our collective approach. We began to look for more ways to help one another and to search for shared solutions that leveraged the diverse range of experience and viewpoints within the team to get there.

Through venture capitalist John Doerr, Google were one of the first cultures to utilise a system called Objectives and Key Results, or OKRs. I know, it's another business acronym, but as a system for monitoring performance and goal achievement it is better than most.

In his book *Work Rules! Insights from Google that will transform how you live and lead*, Google's former Vice President of Operations Laszlo Bock writes,

> Having goals improves performance. Spending hours cascading goals up and down the company, however,

does not. We have a market-based approach, where over time our goals all converge, because the top OKRs are known and everyone else's OKRs are visible.

WHAT IS AN OKR?

An OKR is divided into two parts: a statement of what is to be achieved (objective) and some measurable targets (key results) to help monitor progress towards achieving it. The latter is crucial, because only when you have tangible measures do you make the goal real. The OKR approach requires that you set two to five key results to make it as comprehensive as possible. Oh and words such as *effective* and *efficient* are banned, because they aren't easily measurable. What I like most about OKRs are the following things:

- **Collaboration.** OKRs are set by the team and not done on an individual basis. Therefore they are owned by the team from the outset.

- **Clarity.** OKRs make sense. They're easy to grasp and measure progress in a way that everyone understands. Key results must be based on value, not activity, so they're focused on the end result, not the things to do to get there.

- **Visibility.** Because achievement of OKRs is all about organisational alignment, they are made visible so everyone can see what everyone else is working on and how they're doing.

- **Encourage big goals.** OKRs allow people to dream a little. Bonuses aren't missed as a result of not achieving them, but there's an understanding that aiming high — and being uncomfortable as a result — can lead to big results. These are often referred to as *Moonshots*.

- **Focused.** These are not things to 'set and forget' at the start of the year. They are things that align to the current priorities of the month or quarter and are followed up regularly to assess progress.

Of course, most cultures aren't used to this approach, so it can't be implemented with the click of the fingers, but moving to a team-based approach to goal achievement and recognition can reap huge benefits.

A WORD ON PROJECT BENEFITS

Most cultures will utilise projects to introduce new approaches, products or services throughout their year, and despite trillions being spent (and wasted) on developing the people and processes associated with consistently good delivery, statistically, most will perform poorly—often without consequence for those involved.

Projects (and the cultures required to deliver them) were my life for 20 years and I've written extensively about how to do them well in *The Project Book: The complete guide to consistently delivering great projects*, which is available from all great bookshops ... and some rubbish ones too.

In the section of that book dedicated to senior managers I talk about the big problem projects have with what's known as benefit realisation. A lot of time and effort is spent justifying the 'why' of projects. These business cases often put forward big changes in operational costs, revenue or productivity, yet very few deliver what was promised. This lack of discipline has a significant knock-on effect on morale and plans for the following year. It also erodes the confidence of shareholders and the public, so care needs to be taken to ensure that not only are project benefits achievable, but the discipline ensures that these benefits are realised. There are three reasons why they're not:

1. **Overly optimistic.** When conceptualising projects, senior managers tend to take the 'glass almost full'

approach to the outcomes they expect from projects. This often leads to overly optimistic expectations of the outcomes that will be achieved, which leaves people scratching their heads on how they'll be achieved. In government, they often lie outright—having worked in the public sector for seven years, let me tell you this is rife—in order to get their pet project through an approval process with no hope of ever getting the money back on their investment.

2. **Things change.** As with everything else in our world, things can change in a heartbeat, which means sometimes a particular outcome or benefit expected from a project is no longer achievable. It could be an insurance product, a transport travel time, income expected from a hotel or a result expected from a sports team. This is why expected benefits should be constantly assessed to ensure they remain relevant and achievable, and amended should either of those conditions change. Sunk cost thinking (we've already spent $X so we have to carry on) should be rejected. In his book *Joy Inc.*, Richard Sheridan describes sunk cost reasoning as one of 'the most insidious obstacles to change in business today'.

3. **Don't care enough.** But by far the biggest reason why projects don't achieve the expected outcomes is that those entrusted with ensuring they deliver as promised just don't care enough to see it through. They will appoint people to oversee delivery of the changes, thereby delegating accountability for performance and washing their hands of it. And when, inevitably, the outcomes aren't delivered they avoid any repercussions because, well, cultures just don't care enough. Instead, fingers are pointed at frameworks and processes, rather than at the behaviours of the people involved.

CELEBRATE GOOD TIMES

Where OKRs, goals, deliverables, benefits or outcomes are achieved, then it should be a time of celebration.

In my early working life in England, every celebration involved going to the pub. Well, not every celebration, but most. I was told back then that the team that drinks together, stays together. Thankfully things have moved on (for most). My personal team mantra was always that the team that celebrates together, stays together. And celebration can take many forms, including:

- a simple 'thank you' or 'well done'
- a congratulatory email
- a stand-up or 'town hall' meeting
- morning tea/*la once*/elevenses/*tienuurtje*/*konkelstik*/ *hamarretako*/*arukhat eser* (choose as appropriate)
- a special lunch
- an afternoon event.

However you choose to do it, taking the time to pause and celebrate any kind of achievement is important, as it's an opportunity to praise and show gratitude for the result that's been achieved, rather than showering people with gifts. As Dan Pink says in his book *Drive*, 'Praise and positive feedback are much less corrosive than cash or trophies.'

In great organisational cultures, leaders continually express appreciation for the work that's been done, and when they do this they take care to praise the value demonstrated, behaviour changed or process followed, rather than the person. Chade Meng-Tan explains in his book *Search Inside Yourself*, 'When a person is given process praise (you must have worked hard) it reinforces a growth mindset.'

This is something Carol Dweck talks about in her book *Mindset*, 'If the wrong kind of praise [can lead people] down the path of entitlement, dependence and fragility, maybe the right kinds of praise can lead them down the path of hard work and greater hardiness.'

When done well, celebration, praise and gratitude generate within the culture:

• a greater sense of belonging

• unity around the next target to be achieved

• increased loyalty

• a positive mindset

• reconnection to the values and vision

• improved morale.

If you're working as part of a distributed or remote team, it's important to ensure the work completed by the subcultures is also praised and celebrated. In one of my roles we had a development team based in India and we would schedule our celebratory get-togethers in the late afternoon so we could share the success with our counterparts in Asia by video conference. When a friend of mine was working with a team in Brazil he found it wasn't possible to overcome the time difference, so he sent a recorded video message and they held their celebration at the same time of the day there.

In his book *Creativity Inc.*, Pixar co-founder Ed Catmull advises, 'One of the most crucial responsibilities of leadership is creating a culture that rewards those who lift not just our stock prices but our aspirations as well.'

And one key goal that all staff should aspire to is to make the culture the best it can possibly be.

THE ULTIMATE CULTURAL RECOGNITION AND REWARD

The ultimate reward for having a great culture is to win one of the many awards that recognise and celebrate the best places to be employed. The most prestigious of these is the Fortune 100 Best Companies to Work For™.

This list is compiled from employee responses (as is that from Glassdoor, which also compiles a list of Great Places to Work) to a series of questions describing why the culture is great. The answers are then analysed for size, workforce make-up and what else is happening in their industry or region.

Finally—and most importantly—they assess daily interactions and experiences in relation to vision, values, behaviour, collaboration and innovation.

The process for getting on the list isn't an easy one. There's a highly detailed form to fill in with over 200 data points, a confidential workplace survey, and a team of people working to review news and financial performance to ensure fair play.

It's exhausting just writing about it!

Given all of that, getting on the list is cause for celebration, regardless of where the culture is placed. Obviously more column inches are devoted to the top ten, but any organisation that features on such a list should celebrated wildly. It really is the ultimate recognition and reward that all staff within the culture can receive.

CASE STUDY: National Instruments

National Instruments is a manufacturing organisation headquartered in Austin, Texas. They produce automated test equipment and virtual instrumentation software.

They put continual effort into ensuring not only that they hire for values, but also that they pay fair and equal compensation packages to all staff.

In 2018 they created a cultural development module called 'Recognition is free and unlimited'. Their goal was for people to catch co-workers behaving in a way that offered a role model for others, encouraging positivity and integrating a regular cycle of recognition into their daily practices.

It was one of many such initiatives that led to their being placed eleventh on the 2018 Great Places to Work list.

Obviously, by following all the advice offered in this book, you'll have all you need to make yourself a 'Best Place to Work' case study in the future!

KEY POINTS

- Every person should receive equal recognition for their contribution.

- Goals should be measurable and should be defined by those responsible for achieving them.

- Achievement, however big or small, should be recognised and celebrated.

ACTION YOU CAN TAKE

As well as tackling the bigger issues of pay equity, cultures should take the time to use the OKR approach to define big goals for the subcultures to aim for. Whenever people ask where to start with this, I recommend they search the Atlassian Team Playbook.

Atlassian are teamwork pioneers and go to great lengths to share their cultural 'plays', which work so others have a blueprint to follow. In this spirit they have very kindly granted me a licence to reproduce some of their advice in this book, so here's what they recommend for OKRs.

Setting OKRs: Set the stage (5 minutes)

Introduce the team to the terminology and scoring system. Remind them that OKRs are supposed to be 'uncomfortable'. They won't be fired for setting an ambitious goal and missing it.

Setting OKRs: Choose your objectives (30 minutes)

Pose the question 'What are the most important impacts we need to make in the coming quarter?'

Spend a few minutes brainstorming ideas on sticky notes and posting them on a whiteboard or wall. Group similar ideas together. From there, distil your ideas down to three to five aspirational objectives.

Objectives should be high-level, qualitative statements that are aspirational — not tasks or granular outcomes.

Setting OKRs: Identify your key results (60 minutes)

Identify measurable outcomes that indicate you've achieved your objective.

For each objective, think about the results you would see (and can measure) if you reached it. Again, these are not tasks. These are results.

Assign each KR an owner on the team. If a KR will require collaboration with another team, great! Follow up with them afterwards and make sure they're on board.

Setting OKRs: Amp up your ambition (15 minutes)

Review the objectives and key results you've built out and ask whether they're ambitious enough. If you feel totally confident you can hit a KR, increase the target by ~30 per cent and create a plan to try and hit it. If you're not at all sure you'll hit a KR's target, it's probably set just right.

Make sure the KRs are articulated such that they can be scored on a sliding scale. Hard numbers and percentages work great here.

Also consider whether you have too many or too few Os and KRs. We've found that for a single team of 7–9 people, three objectives with 2–3 ambitious key results each is about right.

Once you have followed these steps it's recommended that you agree the next steps, then plan in regular catch-ups (say, monthly or quarterly) to check on progress — scoring appropriately — so that any issues can be identified early and corrective action taken.

PERFORMANCE MANAGEMENT

Having to deal with employees who behave or perform poorly is something every culture—even 'the number one place to work in the universe'—has to deal with at some stage. More often than not the problem of poor performance has one of two causes: the individual is poorly motivated, or the culture lets the person get away with performing that way.

In the rush to foster harmony and be seen to be fair and tolerant, some cultures are really bad at dealing with poor behaviour and performance; as the saying goes, you're only as good as the behaviour that you walk past. If your culture hopes that by ignoring poor behaviours they'll go away, it should think again. They almost never do, and they have a pernicious impact on people and performance.

Tolerating poor behaviour and performance will inevitably lead to increased stress, anxiety and worry. In *Emotional Intelligence*, Daniel Goleman reported that '126 studies of more than 36,000 people found that the more prone to worry a person is, the poorer their performance, no matter how measured'.

In a Tech Leaders survey from Kapor University in 2017, 78 per cent of employees reported experiencing some form of unfair behaviour or treatment. That's three-quarters of all staff, and of course women experienced or observed significantly more unfairness than men.

The same study also found that:

- nearly a quarter of underrepresented men and women of colour experienced stereotyping, twice the rate of white and Asian men and women
- 1 in 10 women in tech experienced unwanted sexual attention
- LGBT employees were most likely to be bullied (20 per cent) and experience public humiliation or embarrassment (24 per cent).

It's not limited to the technology industry either. Members of Parliament in New Zealand were surveyed in early 2019 on the abuse and harassment they experience. The results were no less damning:

- Fifty-three per cent of women had been the subject of sexist or humiliating comments, and other MPs were commonly the perpetrators.

- Many had suffered rape or death threats from their constituents or other members of the public.

- Crude and sexist comments were passed off as 'part of the culture of Parliament'.

New Zealand's current Prime Minister, Jacinda Ardern, herself admitted that she'd been a victim of sexual harassment and verbal abuse on multiple occasions.

The Speaker of the House has now commissioned a full independent external review, and the outcomes and ramifications of this will be watched carefully around the world as the movement to combat these behaviours gains momentum.

US civil rights activist Tarana Burke was the first to use the 'Me Too' phrase in 2006 to start a campaign of 'empowerment through empathy' among women of colour who had suffered sexual abuse. Actress Alyssa Milano then launched the #MeToo hashtag to draw attention to sexual abuse and harassment in all workplaces. As the movement has grown, things have started to change, but all too slowly.

A poll on sexual harassment commissioned in 2017 by ABC News and *The Washington Post* found that 54 per cent of American women reported receiving 'unwanted and inappropriate' sexual advances, with 95 per cent saying that such behaviour usually went unpunished. Both of those numbers are absolutely appalling. In November of the same year, the Alianza Nacional de Campesinas (the National Farmworkers Women's Alliance) wrote a letter of solidarity to women affected by sexual abuse in Hollywood, and in January 2018 the #TimesUp movement was launched by a group of celebrities to help fund sexual harassment cases around the world.

There are still too many people — predominantly males — in work cultures making excuses and using rhetoric and outdated 'locker room' talk to excuse their behaviour: 'It was a different time then', 'You can't say/do anything anymore', 'It's all gone too PC', as they continue to hold back, humiliate, harass, abuse and demean other human beings. It has to stop.

It's going to take time, courage and resilience, but every culture has to do its bit to guarantee respect and equity in our work practices. There's no precedent for it because it's never been done before. This is the start, and for those looking to evolve their cultures, here is your potential legacy. It's not going to be easy, in fact at times it will be painful, but creating safety and equality for all people should be the number one priority.

The expectations of all members of the culture should be made clear, so no one can hide behind 'Stop being so touchy', 'I was only joking' or 'No one told me'.

As noted in the previous section, this exercise starts with identifying a set of behaviours and describing what it means to demonstrate them. However, if you don't then hold all staff to them (no exceptions) then they are not worth the paper they're written on and the culture will stagnate.

And the impact of poor performance takes its toll.

EVERYONE HAS TO PUT IN A SHIFT

Gallup estimates that over half of the American workforce are disengaged and that this disengagement costs US businesses between $483 billion and $605 billion each year in lost productivity. What lies at the heart of this is the fact that most managers don't know how to motivate employees to get the job done.

In his book *The Five Dysfunctions of a Team*, Patrick Lencioni identifies the fourth dysfunction as 'Avoidance of accountability: The need to avoid interpersonal discomfort prevents team members from holding one another accountable for their behaviours and performance'.

This accountability is missing as a result of three main failures:

1. Managers don't set expectations well.
2. Managers don't understand how to manage and motivate different personalities.
3. Managers don't have the courage to manage poor performance.

Setting expectations well is fundamental to the delivery of any product or service, yet it isn't something that people do very well because, well, like most things, no one showed them how.

I was fortunate. I had my fair share of bad managers early in my career, then in my late twenties I took a new job and found myself reporting to someone whose management style still inspires me today, even though I spent less than two years reporting to him. One of the things he did really well was set expectations.

As a team we were on a pretty tight schedule, which meant every one of us had to bring our best self to work every day and hit the marks we'd been set. I realised early on that to be this kind of person requires discipline and feedback. I needed plenty of both to get the job done and to stretch myself. What I found out very quickly was that everyone does their best work on the edge of uncomfortable. Goals and targets need to be achievable, but if they're too easy or too hard it becomes easy to procrastinate or get distracted. Expectations have to be realistic yet require every ounce of effort to get there.

In my experience, setting expectations well is a four-stage process. This is a skill that every person responsible for managing people needs to excel at; otherwise, when people don't deliver or perform poorly it's extremely difficult to hold them to account, as the expectations weren't clear to begin with.

This is what the process looks like.

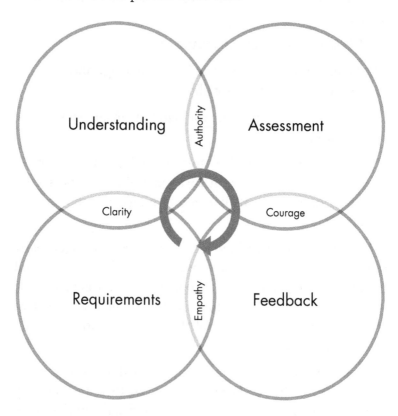

Here's how it works:

- **Requirements**: What's needed? When? What autonomy do they have? Who should they work with? To what level of quality? How often is check-in required? Is any coaching needed?

  Clarity: The requirements should be set using language that is easy to understand. Each set of requirements must be tailored to the employee's personality type. Cut down on jargon, acronyms or technical talk that might confuse.

- **Understanding**: Once the requirements have been outlined, it's important to ensure that the employee fully grasps what's expected and confirms their full understanding.

  Authority: As part of the requirements setting and understanding exercise the manager needs to establish their authority, not in an overbearing, 'I'm in charge' way, but in an 'I'm here to help, so keep me fully informed' way.

- **Assessment**: Whatever the employee's personality type, the manager must check in to ensure progress is being made. Some personalities will require more attention than others.

  Courage: Where progress is not being made, courage will be required as a conversation is needed to bring the work back on track.

- **Feedback**: This is where a conversation is held with the employee to talk about what has and hasn't been done in line with the requirements set. This conversation will be easier if the employee has confirmed their understanding of the requirements.

  Empathy: Empathy is essential in this conversation. The manager's preparation should ensure that the feedback is tailored to the individual and their emotions, and that the requirements are reset accordingly.

While this four-stage process looks straightforward on paper, few managers do it well, or else they fail to provide structured feedback in a way that is helpful. Only 21 per cent of the people interviewed in Gallup's State of the American Workplace survey reported that their performance was managed in a way that motivated them to do outstanding work.

One in five. Wow.

FEEDING BACK ON FEEDBACK

The US Office of Personnel Management has found that early feedback is critical to improving performance. They suggest that the feedback needs to encompass three elements:

- *Specific*—directly relating to the issue at hand (don't dance around it)
- *Timely*—don't wait too long before addressing it
- *Manner*—delivered in a way that will best improve performance.

There is often a fear associated with feedback that really doesn't need to be there. As Mihaly Csikszentmihalyi argues in his book *Flow*, 'Almost any kind of feedback can be enjoyable, provided it is logically related to a goal in which one has invested psychic energy.'

Most managers wait too long to provide this, however, postponing it to the end of the year and the annual ambush (or performance review as it's more formally known). I can't think of many things more unhelpful to cultural evolution or personal development than the following end-of-year conversation:

Manager: You haven't earned your bonus this year as your performance has been rated as only average.

Employee [looking shocked]: But I've hit every target I've been set. Why won't I be getting a bonus?

Manager: We haven't been happy with your behaviour.

Employee [looking even more shocked]: But no one has said anything to me about this all year. Who said my behaviour had been poor?

Manager: I can't tell you that.

Employee [getting angry now]: But how can I provide a contrary viewpoint to defend myself? When did this happen?

Manager: I can't tell you that either.

Such a scenario is utterly ridiculous, yet this sort of conversation is all too common in many cultures that haven't moved away from annual performance reviews!

Writing in *Forbes* magazine, author Liz Ryan lists five reasons that performance reviews are a waste of time:

1. They take up expensive staff hours for no observable gain.

2. Their purpose is unclear.

3. They are unfair.

4. They are insulting.

5. They lack an objective and an outcome.

And if those five reasons aren't enough, consider this. If feedback isn't immediate, then nothing will change or get fixed and the chance for continual personal and cultural improvement is lost.

Adobe, Deloitte and Accenture are examples of organisations that have ditched the annual performance review in favour of a more regular feedback cycle.

Deloitte worked out how many hours the organisation was spending on collating the information relating to performance and holding the review itself. Their finding—which should surprise no one who is still doing it—was that all the preparation time, form-filling, meetings and the nonsense of rating the entire workforce cost them almost 2 million management hours a year!

They also found that most of that time was actually spent talking about the outcomes of the process behind closed doors. Now, I wasn't privy to those meetings, but I can only imagine that they did what others do and grade their people with a view to arriving at even splits across the grades.

A CNBC exposé in early 2019 laid bare Facebook's twice-a-year grading system:

- *Redefine*—the highest grade, achieved by fewer than 5 per cent of employees
- *Greatly exceeds expectations*—10 per cent
- *Exceeds expectations*—35 per cent
- *Meets all*—40 per cent
- *Meets some* (a career-threatening grade)—10 per cent
- *Does not meet*—extremely rare, as people have usually been dismissed before receiving it.

This stack-ranking system—and there are many other similar ones around the world—was invented by Jack Welch in the 1990s and often collects data on a series of key performance indicators. These systems were once seen as the answer; however, as McKinsey concluded in their 2016 paper 'Ahead of the curve: The future of performance management', 'collecting accurate data for 15 to 20 individual indicators can be cumbersome and often generates inaccurate information'. They went on to comment, 'performance-development tools can also identify the top performers more accurately, though everyone already knows subjectively who they are'.

Back to Deloitte and their 2 million hours. The realisation that this much time was being wasted led the company to move to an entirely new model of talking to their people about their performance and career with an emphasis on the future, not the past.

This approach requires honesty and immediate intervention, but once the practice has been used consistently by managers, it's a transformative exercise, as Netflix discovered. In her book *Powerful*, former Chief Talent Officer Patty McCord observes, 'One of the most important insights anyone in business can have is that it's not cruel to tell people the truth respectfully and honestly.' No one benefits from evasion and prevarication, and while I understand that for some personalities this can be difficult, truth-telling is a skill that needs to be learned.

Most important when giving immediate feedback is that it must relate to their behaviour in the context of a particular situation. It can't be based on hearsay or an assumption, or point to a weakness of personality. As Dr Alan Watkins advises in his TED talk 'Being Brilliant Everyday', 'In order to change the result or performance, you have to focus on the behaviour. Most appraisals focus on what you've been doing, not what you need to do.'

One approach I've found extremely useful is SBI (for Situation—Behaviour—Impact). Developed by the Center for Creative Leadership, it is a core part of their coaching framework and looks like this:

- *Situation*—describes the when and where of the incident

- *Behaviour*—describes the behaviour that was directly observed

- *Impact*—describes the impact the behaviour had on other people or its contribution to an objective.

Here is an example of how this might work within a culture:

S: 'During this morning's team meeting …

B: '… you kept interrupting Tash when she was trying to describe the customer requirements.

I: 'I felt this was hugely disrespectful to Tash. It could well have made her feel like she's not being listened to and that what's in your head is more important than anything she has to say.'

Of course, it's also important to praise and show gratitude, and the process can be used in exactly the same way:

S: 'During the speech you gave to the team on Monday ...

B: '... you were calm and confident in your delivery and presented the information in a way that everyone found easy to understand.

I: 'I'm proud of the courage you have shown in developing your public speaking skills, and you have inspired others in the team to follow your example.'

I really like this model because it elevates the values-based behaviours we're looking for individuals within the culture to demonstrate, and at the same time it deals with the negative ones that can be destructive to everything that's being built.

As Daniel Ek, CEO of Spotify, said in an interview in 2018, 'It's super important as a leader to talk about what the culture is and force positive and negative examples continuously.'

CASE STUDY: Netflix

There's simply no way that Netflix's culture could have achieved what it has in such as short space of time if it weren't for its strong approach to setting expectations and managing performance standards. From the outset, they set out to create an organisation where employees understood the organisation's goals, values and behaviours and their personal commitments to upholding these.

Patty McCord relates how they took the time to work with the team to articulate the behaviours at the start, describing what they meant day to day and insisting they be practised until they became consistent.

It was a very bumpy ride in the early years, and we shared with the whole company the difficulties as we encountered them, being very clear about our time frame, our metrics, and what it would take to meet goals.

There were many intense debates, and they constantly ask themselves the question, 'Are we limited by the team we have not being the team we should have?' There's an understanding that spending time coaching others to be better is not always the best option. This might be anathema in most cultures, yet if you want to maintain a high-performing team, you need to lose the people who aren't able to contribute fully to your future goals. Or as McCord puts it, 'We [are] willing to say goodbye to very good people if their skills no longer match the work we need done.'

KEY POINTS

- Deal with poor performance quickly, as the things you walk past will become the norm.
- Become great at setting expectations.
- Provide regular feedback.

ACTION YOU CAN TAKE

Use the expectations model on page 114 to ensure that anyone who has to manage people fully understands how to set their expectations, so the culture can get to a point where they are able to provide regular, honest feedback.

By doing this you can deal with performance management issues quickly before resetting expectations. Being unclear about what's expected gives poor-performing employees an excuse and also sends a negative message to those within the culture who are doing their utmost to take it forward.

If someone doesn't have the skills to deliver on the goals the culture has set, a process must be followed to move that person on.

But gratitude should also be shown; otherwise, it will feel like it's always bad news, and continually cutting and replacing people isn't good for stability. A delicate balance is required, but without it the culture will either stagnate or become combatant — and the good staff will leave. That's the last thing any culture needs.

DIVERSITY & INCLUSION

There's a quote I love by American civil rights campaigner and poet Maya Angelou: 'It is time for parents to teach young people early on that in diversity there is beauty and there is strength.' As parents of two young children, my wife and I feel a responsibility to ensure that our little people don't ever see diversity and inclusion as an add-on in life. It should come naturally. It should never be a program or a series of quotas. It's not a 'nice to have', something to 'work on' or a mandated policy. It should be inherent in all cultures as we move to an environment that revolves around networks, community, shared learning and strong values.

As I have discussed, being clear on the cultural values sets the tone for everything else. Values underpin the behaviours of individuals, bring people together, and create the foundation for collaboration, creativity and recruitment.

Where there are strong values, diversity of experience, ideas and opinion are sought after. Where there's a sense of belonging, people feel they're able to share without judgement or prejudice.

Many blogs and articles speak of this as the workplace of the future, yet it should exist now. Netflix asserts: 'Organisations talk about diversity being the most important thing, but then never make it a priority and go with quick-fix policies instead.' All people should feel welcomed and encouraged to contribute.

Atlassian's 2018 State of Diversity report, which focused primarily on the lack of diversity in the technology sector, found that even though there was an increased number of people from underrepresented groups among their US respondents, the figure is still much less than a third, at 26 per cent. The same respondents also said that their company needed no improvement in the areas of age, gender, race/ethnicity and sexual orientation.

In the report, they put this down to three factors:

1. **Diversity fatigue.** People are over endless initiatives that don't deliver results.

2. **The wrong conversation.** The initiatives often focus on representation numbers rather than on 'belonging' within the organisation.

3. **Breadth of issues.** There's a sense of overwhelm and 'what can I do?' when it comes to believing they can make a difference.

There's still much work to do to ensure there is fair and equal representation within cultures. Workplaces should reflect the community they support, and while the naysayers in your culture might say 'not in my lifetime', it's everyone's collective responsibility to start the change process. Still not convinced? Here are some more damning statistics:

- Only 25 women are CEOs of Fortune 500 companies (5 per cent).

- There are just five BAME (Black, Asian and Minority Ethnic) managers across 92 professional English football clubs (5.4 per cent), despite more than 30 per cent of players being of BAME background.

- Only 2.5 per cent of Google's workforce is black.

- Nearly a quarter of underrepresented men and women of colour experience stereotyping, twice the rate of white and Asian men and women.

In 2017, Sheryl Sandberg, in conjunction with McKinsey & Company, produced a 'Women in the Workplace' research report. Among its findings was that one-third of organisations still don't have a strategy for hiring from underrepresented groups. Additionally, 36 per cent of organisations aren't checking their job advertisements and descriptions for biased language, and 28 per cent don't use clear and consistent language for every candidate.

Kieran Snyder is the founder and CEO of an organisation called Textio. She completed a doctorate in linguistics and cognitive science before working for Microsoft and, briefly, Amazon. She established Textio in 2014 to help organisations use data analytics to uncover patterns in language that cause people not to respond to job ads.

The results that cultures have been able to gain by using Textio have been staggering. Johnson & Johnson had 90 000 more women apply for roles than it did prior to using Snyder's tool. Atlassian increased the number of women in the engineering cohort by 47 per cent in two years and the number of black and Latino technical interns to 33 per cent.

Of course, bias isn't restricted to language but is reflected in action too.

As cultures evolve to create this optimal employee experience and mix, codes of conduct will be required to ensure that individuals who display negative bias are coached and that those who are unwilling to change are managed out.

When talking to Dom Price at Atlassian, I asked him what was the hardest thing for new people to do when they joined Atlassian. He told me a personal story of when he himself joined that's applicable to most people who've never worked anywhere as diverse and inclusive as Atlassian.

The toughest thing he had to do, he said, was to unlearn some of the things he'd been taught how to do at other, less forward-thinking cultures. In order to change and become less rigid in his own thinking and acting, he had to learn how to become curious and ask questions. Lots of questions.

In another interview he said, 'We care about other levels of diversity... but we get the most amount of value from cognitive diversity.'

BIAS AND COGNITIVE DIVERSITY

When I work with older generation cultures (although this issue is not limited to them) I tell them that the hardest thing they'll need to work on with regard to improving the way they do things is challenging their existing thinking—or biases—as these are the things that can often get in the way.

Consciousness, or the state of being aware and responsive to one's surroundings, has been studied for hundreds of years. It is the relationship between our senses and how we perceive the physical world, and the way the brain interprets that information. There have been many theories of consciousness—from the Mayans to René Descartes—and today neurologists and psychologists continue to seek a better understanding of it.

Social psychologists see consciousness as a product of cultural influence and believe that individuals have little say in it. Erin Mayer, in her book *The Culture Map*, supports this view. Through her research on organisational working cultures she has found that our powers of persuasion and influence are profoundly affected by the culture in which we live and work.

Sigmund Freud's theory on consciousness is arguably the best known. He proposed three levels of consciousness:

1. *Unconscious*—essentially a store of emotions, feelings, needs and urges outside of our conscious awareness that are hard to retrieve but can greatly influence our behaviour. There's good stuff and bad stuff here.

2. *Preconscious*—a layer of memories or recollections just below our conscious mind that can easily be recalled

3. *Conscious*—things we are thinking about at any given point in time. It's what we can talk about calmly, logically and rationally right now.

To illustrate his point he drew an iceberg showing how the conscious mind above the surface can be greatly influenced by the unconscious and preconscious mind below. 'Properly speaking,' he said,

> the unconscious is the real psychic; its inner nature is just as unknown to us as the reality of the external world, and it is just as imperfectly reported to us through the data of consciousness as is the external world through the indications of our sensory organs.

Although he also is alleged to have said, 'Sometimes a cigar is just a cigar', so there's that.

In today's cultures, programs are undertaken to help people better understand their unconscious biases so they find it easier to unlearn some things in order to help them move forward. This involves helping individuals to challenge the traditional ways they may act or think about things and to explore contrary views, thus embracing greater diversity of thought by asking 'why?' and 'why not?' more often.

For a working culture the benefits of this cognitive diversity—the inclusion of different problem-solving and thinking styles—can be huge. Much greater than those offered by the more common kinds of diversity—race, sex, age—that cultures often prioritise. Research at the Harvard Business School in 2017 found that these kinds of diversity did not correlate with a team's results, but that cognitive diversity most assuredly did.

Google's Scott E. Page understands diversity and inclusion better than most. He is a social scientist and Leonid Hurwicz Collegiate Professor of Complex Systems, Political Science, and Economics at the University of Michigan. He also wrote many books on diversity before it became fashionable for HR departments to talk about it. His most recent book, *The Diversity Bonus: How great teams pay off in the knowledge economy*, discusses and demonstrates the benefits that a more diverse team can bring to a culture.

Page focuses predominantly on cognitive diversity, although he sees it as closely interwoven with gender diversity. In an article for Princeton University in 2017, he said, 'Identity diversity refers to differences in race, gender, sexual orientation, ethnicity, physical capabilities, and culture. Cognitive diversity refers to differences in information, knowledge bases, representations, categories, heuristics, causal models, and frameworks.' Further, 'our identities consist of multiple dimensions that collectively influence what we know, how we see, and how we think.'

He cautions against one-dimensional frames of reference such as 'a woman's perspective' and talks about how the best teams are made of diverse thinkers. While he admits that diversity bonuses may not be realised from routine tasks such as packing boxes, in highly complex scenarios cultures can expect:

- improved problem-solving
- increased innovation
- more accurate predictions.

All of which lead to better performance and results.

Cultures that strive for harmony over difference end up with groupthink. William H. Whyte first coined this term in a *Fortune* magazine article in 1952. In 1972 Yale psychologist Irving Janis developed groupthink theory. He defined groupthink as a 'deterioration in mental efficiency, reality testing and moral judgments as a result of group pressures', referring to the Bay of Pigs fiasco and the Japanese attack on Pearl Harbor as two historical case studies.

Writing in *Psychology Today*, Sara Canaday summed up the dangers of groupthink in a cultural context: 'A culture that encourages conformity of thought breeds stagnation.'

Of course, having a diverse team isn't the answer to every cultural problem. Team members have to work really hard to ensure that connections are built and maintained. Like most things within a culture it will be seen as 'hard work' and something that has to be done over and above their day job. In fact, greater diversity often leads to greater conflict. In these situations, it's important to ensure that people remain true to the values of the culture, not their own ideas, as this is how problems are resolved.

INCLUSION

Creating a culture that is diverse in its people and its thinking is one thing, but you also need to ensure that everyone is given a voice and is listened to. Not a platform for preaching, but an opportunity to share and to contribute to solutions.

This is something I talked about at the start of the book. Most organisational cultures fail to evolve because the employees — and the people who invest in the culture — aren't given an opportunity to contribute to its definition. As a result, whether they mean to or not, they exclude people. It's not just about culture definition, though. Some other ways to make people feel excluded are:

- executives flying business class while everyone else flies economy

- training budgets (but not executives' pet projects) being cut when money is tight

- expensive off-sites for executives only

- favouring the viewpoint of specialists instead of canvassing others' opinions

- taking things 'offline'

- spending money on external consultants when the expertise exists in house.

People and Culture specialists Culture Amp and Paradigm produced the first inclusion report for the tech industry, '6 Ways to Foster Belonging in the Workplace', for which they surveyed over 7000 people from 35 organisations. Despite how differently people from different demographics viewed culture, they discovered that 'belonging' was the common metric that motivated, inspired and instilled a sense of pride in people at work. They defined belonging as 'the feeling of security and support when there is a sense of acceptance, inclusion, and identity for a member of a certain group or place'.

There are some great insights in the report that are not just specific to the tech industry. Indeed, I have shared it with many of my former colleagues still working in government, and even with my daughter's football coach!

I specifically like the section 'Be intentional about inclusion', as it had me recalling how the different organisations I've worked for did this. Here are some examples of simple things we did in order to be more inclusive (none were perfect solutions in isolation, but all contributed to the way our people felt about the organisation):

- **No secret projects.** While there were some things (specifically around restructuring) we couldn't talk about in detail, we knew that if we kept the fact that it was being planned secret it would lead to an erosion of trust and Chinese whispers, so we were always as open and honest as we could possibly be.

- **Priority list.** Along with our strategy, we would publish our annual list of priorities that had been approved by the senior management team. Every time a priority changed we would republish it.

- **Shared documents.** We introduced shared documents as a way of improving collaboration. A training program was required. The senior management team were part of this, but everyone's contribution was treated equally seriously.

- **Monthly presentations.** Every month two people were invited to senior management team meetings to present on initiatives they were working on and how the senior management team could help.

- **Annual off-sites.** Off-sites were limited to one a year, and members of different teams were invited to them to provide their insights on what we might have missed or not thought about.

Above all, however, was a sense of humanity. We encouraged people to tell stories and share ideas, and we wouldn't tolerate brilliant jerks. We recognised human fallibility and embraced diverse opinions to ensure that everyone felt valued not only for the job they did, but for the contributions they made to the conversation.

Spotify's Code of Conduct and Ethics has this to say about inclusion:

> The diversity of Spotify's employees is a tremendous asset. We come from all around the world and represent a variety of cultures, experiences and diverse backgrounds. We strive to create and maintain an inclusive work environment in which all of our employees are treated with dignity, decency and respect.

Dignity, decency and respect. Doesn't everyone deserve this?

No one, in my experience, enters their working environment having chosen to be the worst version of themselves and to look for ways to get in the way of progress. There are many factors that contribute to such a mindset and the actions it leads to. The culture has a role to play in ensuring that these issues are dealt with empathetically. Waiting for a leader to sort it out creates a bottleneck and reinforces the command and control structure that many people are striving to move away from.

To create a culture of citizenship and community is to make an investment that will pay huge dividends. It will always trump policy and procedure and help cultures move from box ticking to belonging.

CASE STUDY: Intuit

Intuit are a tech company based in Mountain View, California, that principally sells financial and accounting software. They were founded in 1983 and have almost 9000 employees worldwide. They have developed many incredible programs around diversity and inclusion, and regularly publish statistics on every element of their workforce, including on gender, ethnicity and pay. Here's a snapshot of three other initiatives:

- **Intuit Again**. This program was introduced in India in 2013 and provides opportunities to return to work following a career break. For many women, returning to the workforce having made the decision to pause their career for family reasons can be especially difficult. Intuit recognises how tough it can be, both emotionally and from a skills perspective, to step back up. This program helps them to restart their careers from where they left off, and to rebuild their confidence too.

- **Diversapalooza**. This week-long forum focuses on how diversity and inclusion improves innovation. Community leaders are invited to share their thoughts with Intuit staff and management on how the organisation can continue to grow and embrace difference. There is a focus on creativity throughout, with Hispanic and Latino artists sharing their stories and a Pride Network booth for members of the team to share how they bring the best version of themselves to their work.

- **Week of service**. In 2013 the San Diego office decided to spend a week volunteering together and giving back to the local community. This activity has since been extended to the rest of the workforce and become a significant company event. In 2018 alone more than 14 000 hours of volunteer time and almost US$350 000 were donated to those in need.

KEY POINTS

- Remove any kind of bias from your hiring practices.

- Encourage differences in thought and opinion.

- Develop a sense of belonging by removing activities that might alienate people.

ACTION YOU CAN TAKE

Diversity and inclusion are an important aspect of cultural strategy. While training in some areas may be required, ultimately it's the little things that make the difference. Running a survey is one way of finding out how connected people feel to the culture, but if their comments aren't actioned then it's just another empty gesture that will make them feel excluded.

Take the time to analyse and compare the pay of male and female staff, then publish what you have found as a way of providing accountability and driving action for change where required. You can also follow Buzzfeed's lead and publish stats on how diverse the workforce is.

Use a tool such as Textio to remove any kind of bias from your job advertising. This is a very simple thing you can do immediately.

PILLAR 5
COLLABORATION

There's a current trend (among the many I've mentioned in this book) of managers in underperforming cultures talking about the importance of collaboration as if they've just found a Golden Ticket in a well-known fictional chocolate bar. Like it's never been a part of great teams before, and if they could only unlock the secret to doing it well they'd be successful, like, forevs.

So to reinforce the importance of collaboration they do the one thing guaranteed to ensure they never get there. They *talk* about it. All the time. They need to collaborate on this, increase collaboration on that and cross-collaborate on the other.

When talking about it doesn't work, they try copying others who collaborate well. Not by implementing a strong vision, defining a set of values or holding people to agreed behaviours, but by changing the names of the teams. More about that in a bit.

But make no mistake, collaboration—or the way people work together—is critical to a culture's success. It's just that most cultures aren't very good at it. In the 2018 Deloitte 'Human Capital Trends' report, 94 per cent of organisations said that 'agility and collaboration are critical to their organisation's success', yet only 6 per cent said they were where they need to be today.

Google's 2015 'Working Together Better' report talked extensively about the importance of collaboration and its positive impact on both culture and results. For example, 88 per cent who strongly agreed that their culture fostered collaboration also said that morale was high. High morale = happy staff = improved culture = greater productivity = better results. Okay, so it's not quite as simple as that, but you get the idea of how important collaboration is.

Before I crack on with this discussion, let's be clear about what collaboration isn't. It is not:

- endless consultation
- consensus
- harmony
- striving for perfection
- complex sign-off processes
- sending out long emails copying everyone in
- back-to-back meetings.

Most of these things actually get in the way of collaboration. They often create divisions and lead to disillusionment and disengagement. Some cultures spend so long trying to keep their people happy that they upset everyone and any hope of collaboration is lost.

One of my favourite lines from the 2015 Netflix culture deck is this: 'We're a team, not a family. We're like a pro sports team, not a kids' recreational team. Netflix leaders hire, develop and cut smartly so we have stars in every position.'

'One reason Reed and I started using the "team not family" metaphor,' explains Patty McCord in her book *Powerful*, 'was that as the company kept changing, we saw that nostalgia for the good old scrappy days was a powerful force of resistance.' Nostalgia inspires ideas of former harmony; as a result cultures lose their edge and protectionism gets in the way of progress.

Another good example of this came out of the recent Prudential Inquiry into the Commonwealth Bank of Australia, which found that 'Overly complex and bureaucratic decision-making processes that favoured collaboration over timely and effective outcomes slowed the detection of risk failings.'

More consultation in the hope of harmony will always, inevitably get in the way of progress.

Great cultures don't force collaboration between individuals. They create the foundations—through their vision, values and behaviours—and let the team forge its own way. As if working with a piece of clay on a potter's wheel the team then turn it, build it and shape it until it's fit for purpose, whatever that might be. But they recognise that even though they have an agreement on *how* to work together, good collaboration means continually looking for better and smarter ways to do things.

Each culture has to ensure that its people not only have the skills to do this, but that a supportive and trusting system exists to allow them to do it.

As Gerd Gigerenzer says in his book *Gut Feelings: The intelligence of the unconscious*, 'If an organisation doesn't support a goal of creating an environment of collaboration, then it tends to fall apart or never gets off the ground in the first place.'

Simply identifying people to work together and telling them to collaborate doesn't work. This is an area where good leadership—as discussed under 'Behaviour'—has a crucial role to play. These 'captains of culture' ensure that time and space are created to reach agreement on the principles of collaboration *before* any work starts and that people are genuinely interested not only in the role they have to play, but also in the objective. Self-motivation is crucially important here, but so is a catalyst to ensure there is energy and commitment from all involved. This is the fuel for the collaboration fire, and to be successful the fire cannot be allowed to extinguish itself.

In highly engaged cultures, leadership doesn't rest with one individual; it is a shared responsibility that passes seamlessly between people, depending on the task or situation at hand. A report published in *Psychology Today* in July 2017 noted, 'Study after study has shown that teams are more creative and productive when they can achieve high levels of participation, cooperation, and collaboration among members.' This requires that every member take a turn in the lead. As discussed under 'Personality & communication', this may require some people to 'step outside themselves', but in highly engaged cultures this is much easier to do as you know you have the full support of those around you.

THE FLATTER THE STRUCTURE, THE BETTER

One way to help people to collaborate is to remove all barriers—perceived or real—to doing so, including the dreaded and outdated structure chart. Nothing screams command and control more than an organisational chart with a manager at the top and workers at the bottom. The surviving royal houses around the world still depend on rigid hierarchies of precedence and privilege, but such divisions have no relevance in the forward-thinking cultures of today.

Not least because a vertical hierarchy doesn't represent how work actually takes place. Responsibility for decision making rests with groups of subcultures within the larger organisational culture. They collaborate on the best way to complete their work, then interact with other subcultures to ensure the outcomes are achieved.

Ridding oneself of a hierarchical view of people is an effective way to start the process of moving towards a forward-thinking, ever-evolving culture. This is something Spotify identified early in their cultural journey, when they moved to smaller, empowered teams that took full responsibility for their work and outcomes. These 'Squads', as they are known, co-locate, agree on their cultural principles, choose the methods they'll use to deliver, and are trusted to define their own goals and outcomes.

In these non-hierarchical, 'self-organising' teams, different people step up to facilitate discussions and lead work as required. The model below illustrates the shift from structured to flexible leadership.

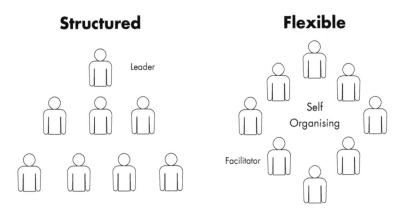

This model puts the emphasis on the continuous improvement of people and products, ensuring a better outcome for the customer and the organisation.

In his book *Team of Teams*, General Stanley McChrystal comments, 'Where org charts are tidy... teams are messy.' His very valid point was that it's one thing to draw a structure, but collaboration requires different people talking to different people at different times; to be truly effective it can't rely on single points of failure at the top. It was a shift that he acknowledged was necessary but nonetheless made him uncomfortable. 'As an instinctive perfectionist, it pained me to do it, but I began pushing authority further down the chain of command.'

When self-organising subcultures take the time to create efficient networks that share information, work and celebrate success together, collaboration is highly effective and everyone benefits.

Deloitte noted in its 2017 'Human Capital Trends' report, 'Real day-to-day work takes place in networks, not teams', an idea they doubled down on in their 2018 report: 'The organisation of the future is moving away from hierarchies and towards networks.'

SAFETY FOR ALL

For these networks to be creative, proactive and productive, they need to provide a safe environment in which people can do their best work. After surveying more than 180 of their teams, Google found this to be the number one attribute out of 250. That's how important it is.

The Social Cognitive Neuroscience Lab at UCLA's Department of Psychology, Psychiatry and Biobehavioural Science concluded that the human need for belonging was perceived as even more important than food, water and shelter. Cultural evolutions that aren't handled well almost always reduce psychological safety, as they threaten the status of individuals while offering no protection from the *threat* of change.

Author Fiona Robertson observed that,

> things that have made us belong and be welcome and accepted here, might start to be frowned upon. If that were to happen, then we may risk losing the belonging we have worked so hard to earn. This is interpreted by our brains as a significant threat to our survival.

Amy C. Edmondson, whose work I have followed for a number of years now, is an authority on *psychological safety* (PS). In a paper in 1999 she described it like this: 'Psychological safety describes the collective belief of how team members and leaders respond when another member "puts themselves on the line", by asking a question, reporting an error, or raising a difficult issue.'

In short, can people do their jobs without insecurity, embarrassment or threat of reprisal? If the answer is no to any of these questions, then a culture of psychological safety does not exist.

I've read a lot of blogs and articles recently about creating an optimal staff experience, and while some haven't specifically mentioned PS, this idea usually sits at the core. We are, after all, at the start of a movement towards more human-centred design in just about every area of our lives, and this includes our work culture.

In 2012, Amy Edmondson recommended four useful ways in which cultures can increase PS, and I have expanded on each of these with my own ideas on how to do them well:

1. **Accessibility.** This relies on people within the culture being approachable. They don't dismiss people who seek an opinion or a decision or wish to share information. People are treated empathetically and with a warmth that encourages further interaction.

2. **Invite participation by admitting fallibility.** People like to see expressions of vulnerability. Admitting to mistakes made and acknowledging you aren't the smartest person in the room with all the answers encourages others to share and contribute. It also helps to build strong, supportive relationships.

3. **Frame failures as learning opportunities.** Blame is rife in cultures that lack PS, especially when scapegoats are

sought for failure. Failure is a natural, even necessary human tendency, without which innovation cannot thrive. By changing the narrative from one of failure to one of learning, the blame culture is diminished and people's fear of making mistakes is removed.

4. **Set boundaries and hold people accountable.** Creating clear, unambiguous boundaries for people to work within encourages them to speak up without fearing they will be seen as ignorant or incompetent. It will also give them the confidence to challenge others who step outside these boundaries.

One exercise I've run with subcultures is to challenge them to define the things they'll do to demonstrate Edmondson's four principles in their own environment. It's a simple yet effective way of getting a group to create a view of what PS means to them, rather than have someone else tell them.

SAVE POLITICS FOR THE POLITICIANS

In one of my government jobs I was told that in order to progress I had to master the art of politics. Of course I'd heard of 'office politics', but I didn't really know what it meant, but was told that it was critical to my success. So obviously my first question was, 'What do you mean?'

I was told—and I'm definitely paraphrasing here, and removing the expletives—that it's the skill of influencing people in order to gain a change that you're looking for. I remember a meeting in my first week at which I was told how to 'play senior managers off against each other'. I dutifully took notes, wondering what I'd walked into.

Not long into the job I found out I was going head to head with people who were telling a slightly different version of the story I was telling in order to get what they needed out of a situation and to make my approach appear less persuasive. It wasn't that they were lying (well, not always); it's just that they were better at subjective narrative than I was.

It all started to feel like the Rashomon effect. In the 1950 Japanese period film *Rashomon* directed by Akira Kurosawa, a murder/suicide occurs and four different, contradictory versions of the story are given by four different people. Crucially all four are presented in a completely plausible way, so you really had no idea what was true. I won't spoil it for you but it was the first Japanese film to have worldwide appeal, such was its impact.

If you're looking for a less gruesome example of the principle, watch *Alvin and the Chipmunks: Chipwrecked*. It's amazing what you can learn when you spend a Sunday afternoon on the sofa watching TV with the kids.

But I digress. To cut a long story short, I didn't stay in that job very long. The culture really wasn't great and try as I might with the team, we just couldn't influence a change in the positive (non-political) way we wanted and almost all of us left, disappointed but with almost a year of valuable learning.

Some people will tell you that office politics is unavoidable and a natural part of any culture. These people are wrong. Dead wrong. These are people who have mastered the art, but are likely to be found out when the culture is honest, ethical and holds its people to account for what is said and done both inside and outside the office.

Office politics creates divisions and drags down emotionally intelligent people.

When evolving your culture, coach and mentor those who seek to use power, influence and spin to get what they want; if that doesn't work, get rid of them altogether. Their values definitely won't align with those of the culture as a whole.

That said, people should still be encouraged to undertake internal networking and relationship building with those from whom they can learn (as Spotify do with their Guilds), but in an emotionally intelligent way that isn't manipulative and self-serving.

CASE STUDY: Hospital trauma teams

Hospital emergency departments are a good place to find great collaboration as the staff have to work quickly in highly stressful situations where they must make life or death decisions. Serious trauma events and road traffic accidents account for more than 10 per cent of deaths worldwide, and this figure would be significantly higher were it not for the dedication and collaboration of healthcare professionals.

Writing in the UK *Nursing Times*, Lee Turner, Timothy Hodgetts and Gary Kenward outlined the collaboration required between different networks of people in order to react quickly to trauma cases.

Trauma teams have to be established quickly. 'The allocation of roles within the team before the arrival of patients and knowledge of how the team will work are essential.' The advice of the Royal College of Surgeons at the time was that a consultant must be the leader, but in practice that wasn't the case. 'The specialty of the leader is not important as long as he or she is committed to the role.'

A team has to prepare and check the equipment and systems required (for instance, fluids have to be warmed prior to use), and systematic approaches to managing patients have to be agreed up front to ensure that nothing is missed.

The nursing team has a critical role to play in supporting the trauma team, taking responsibility for:

- pain management
- patient monitoring
- communication with relatives
- controlling environmental factors such as health and safety regulations.

And often all of this groundwork has to be done in minutes, not hours. There's no time for people to be precious about structures or position, or for complex communications. The consequences of any procrastination could be catastrophic.

KEY POINTS

- Collaboration can't be forced.
- Removing layers and structures enables greater collaboration.
- Politics and poor communication obstruct collaboration.

ACTION YOU CAN TAKE

In small groups, ask people to come up with statements that define *how* they will work together. I have listed some examples below (though they must be fit for purpose, aligning with what the culture is trying to achieve or overcome):

- We have the courage to deal with our issues face to face.
- We use our time together productively.

- We commit fully to the goals we set ourselves.

- We act empathetically at all times, but don't carry passengers.

These principles of group accountability then become the foundation for hourly, daily, weekly and monthly collaboration, and are used to ensure that the energy, spirit and determination captured when defining them is maintained. They become the glue that holds the team together, the criteria used for hiring new people into the culture, and the basis for moving people on to keep individuals challenged and the team fresh.

You can also get members of subcultures together to agree on a safe team charter based on Amy Edmondson's four ways to increase psychological safety.

PROCESS & COMPLIANCE

Having a process is important, but only if it adds value to what you're trying to achieve. People's behaviours and discipline need to be good, there need to be high levels of trust for people to follow and a feedback loop to ensure that it's fit for purpose.

Of course, how you think about process will depend largely on your personality. Some people like it more than others. It's in their DNA and they're always going to want it. I'm not one of those people. I believe you need just enough process for people to feel empowered to make decisions, and no more.

Often the first signs you get about the process culture are revealed when you're hired.

Lars Schmidt, founder of Amplify, suggested in a *FastCompany* article that 'the hiring process should reflect the people skills that you're on the hunt for', yet how many times have you waited, waited and waited for an offer, or any kind of communication, only to have to sheepishly follow up to find out if you were still wanted. And that doesn't take into account the nonsense you often see when setting up a time to be interviewed!

Something I hear a lot is, 'If we didn't have process, we wouldn't get things done.' Which really says a lot about not only the culture of the organisation but those paid more money than most to be its custodians.

I found this mindset was rife in the government departments I worked in, with their swim lanes, stage gates, four levels of business case, three levels of plan, 16-column spreadsheets for risk identification, two pages of signatures, acronym dictionaries and 100-page PowerPoint presentations.

Lots of organisations have similar nonsensical processes; it's not unique to government. The manager of one sports team I spoke with in the US had to have a prospective addition to the squad approved by seven people before he could even approach an agent for the player in question! On more than one occasion they missed out on an acquisition because of this process.

Unfortunately, as noted by L. David Marquet in his excellent book *Turn the Ship Around*, 'When it comes to processes, adherence to the process frequently becomes the objective, as opposed to achieving the objective that the process was put in place to achieve.'

There's a word for this kind of approach and it's not a good one. Bureaucracy. It's even hard to spell, which signals how hard it makes everything.

Bureaucracy exists everywhere. In his book *Creativity Inc.*, Ed Catmull talks about how Pixar started to stifle its own creativity through increased process. '"Trust the process" morphed into "assume that the process will fix things for us".' Alluding to the impact that too many steps can have on a culture and its creativity, Brad Bird, who directed the Pixar movies *The Incredibles* and *Ratatouille*, commented, 'The process either makes you or unmakes you.'

In bureaucratic cultures, adherence to a process, regardless of how dumb it might be, becomes the objective and common sense is often shot down by people who demand consistency. What needs to be consistent is not adherence to the process, however, but the behaviours of the people.

In bureaucratic cultures, the process is almost always not the problem; the people and their attitude towards the process are. Left unchecked, these people will demand more words, longer documents, different formats, more buzzwords, acronyms and confusing language, and that it's all done 'in line with corporate branding guidelines'.

I'm starting to use this book as a personal therapy session. *The Culture Diaries*, as it were:

Monday, 27 March 2003

Just completed the capacity and capability BC2 revision. Feedback from AB was that it was incoherent almost to the point of incomprehensible and that further revisions were required before it can be presented to the IMTGCT for Governance Review 3 (GR3) and passed to the IT Central Unit (ICU) for consultation 1 (C1). A separate PowerPoint pack (min. 30 pages — must adhere to corporate branding) will need to be produced.

Tuesday, 28 March 2003

Resigned.

When it comes to compliance with legislation, a certain amount of paperwork is unavoidable in order to demonstrate the why, what and how to auditors acting on behalf of the regulating body. Rarely, however, is the regulating body asked directly what the requirement is. Instead, assumptions are made, fiefdoms formed and the endless collection of words and data begins.

In one of my government roles I had the unenviable role of being the conduit between our division and the regulator. We were audited twice a year and a cloud of fear seemed to gather over the team as the time approached. I couldn't quite understand it.

Three months into my role I requested a meeting with the regulator to discuss what was expected of us, over and above what was set out in the guidance notes. Apparently a face-to-face meeting to discuss expectations was unprecedented and the regulator didn't quite know how to respond. He invited three other people (for safety, I assumed) and said they would assume responsibility for documenting the outcomes.

Over the course of 45 minutes I questioned every ambiguous statement in the guidance notes until I was crystal clear on what the *actual* requirements were. As a result of that conversation, we were able to cut back by almost two-thirds what was previously submitted, and we received a glowing report at our next audit.

Risk management often tends to succumb to a complicated bureaucratic approach, which results in endless amounts of risk logging (spreadsheets, forms, reports) and very little in the way of risk management.

Taking calculated risks is crucial for any culture regardless of what it does and where in the world it is situated. This is especially true when evolving a culture. Most organisations can become paralysed by the thought of risk and spend weeks and months waiting for the 'right' conditions. Of course, those risks may be realised or they may not. That's why they're called 'risks' and not 'issues'.

Uncertainty can lead to procrastination, which will eventually lead to stagnation of a culture. Risk management requires just enough analysis to understand the consequences of doing or not doing something, then a decision needs to be made. You may fill in a form to track the progress of this decision, but doing so is not the process. Making the decision is.

Too many cultures tie themselves in knots trying to document every thought in every step of a decision-making process, when what's required is simplicity and common sense. For these cultures, process hides poor behaviour and never fixes it.

This is not news to most, yet many cultures not only refuse to simplify things, but keep on adding to their complexity. Research firm Gartner talked about this in a paper in 2015, declaring, 'Organisations' refusal to address complexity in the business process is a main reason for failure.'

One set of guidelines that every culture should have is a code of conduct to ensure that everyone understands what's expected of them—behaviourally, morally and ethically. Great cultures keep this short and sweet, as they hire people who already model these behaviours. For everyone else, there are tomes of information that are easy to ignore or be confused by, then every now and then someone will fall foul of an advisory and HR will send out a reminder to every employee about what it means in the context of their culture.

Put simply, it requires being health and safety conscious, following recruitment and people guidelines, having the organisation's best interests at heart during contractual negotiations, being transparent and honest in supplier dealings, not taking 'kickbacks' or 'favours', and understanding the law.

Patty McCord, formerly of Netflix, recommends in her book *Powerful*, 'You should operate with the leanest possible set of policies, procedures, rules, and approvals, because most of these top-down mandates hamper speed and agility.' Or, as one CEO of a company I'm working with told staff at a town hall meeting, 'If what you're doing is going to compromise the company in any way or may break the law, you need to talk to a manager; otherwise, let us know how you get on.'

At Atlassian they have HR guides for the 'grown-up stuff', but they don't document things as decrees. When you have a cognitively diverse workforce who've been hired for their values and behaviours, then you can take a more informal and mature approach and avoid becoming a top-heavy bureaucracy.

Thankfully, with the shift to more agile or flexible ways of working, we're seeing more of these bureaucratic towers being pulled down.

AGILITY IS NOT A SHORT CUT

The agile movement was born in 2001 when 17 software developers got together to share stories and ideas on how to free themselves from the autocratic command and control processes of the eighties and nineties. All they wanted to do was code, and to be trusted to do the right thing by the organisations they worked for. Their ideas were comprehensively captured in the Agile Manifesto.

What the manifesto called for was for people to work together in self-organising teams to release working software every two weeks. They wanted to keep it simple so it could easily be added to in future iterations, and above all to let the teams choose any process they wished to make this happen.

And that meant a reduction, or in some cultures an eradication, of the bureaucratic ways of the past. McKinsey noted in its paper 'How to Create an Agile Organisation',

'Only 29 percent of bureaucratic respondents, for example, report following rapid iteration and experimentation, while 81 percent of agile respondents say the same.'

My favourite statement in the Agile Manifesto is often overlooked, yet it nicely sums up the foundations required for a flexible and swift approach to delivery to work: 'It's about delivering good products to customers by operating in an environment that does more than talk about "people as our most important asset" but actually "acts" as if people were the most important.'

In other words, cultures need to free people from the shackles of process and trust them to deliver. Expectations must still be set correctly and value must be provided in what's delivered, but beyond that people are left to get on with it.

This can be challenging for cultures that are coming from a position of command and control, and we're already seeing 'agile' ways of working being implemented as methods and processes in their own right, which is the antithesis of what was called for in the original manifesto.

One of the original manifesto signatories and a founder of the XP (Extreme Programming) software development approach, Ron Jeffries, has expressed horror at this development. In a 2018 blog he called for software developers to abandon this version of agile, commenting, 'I really am coming to think that software developers should have no adherence to any "Agile" method of any kind. [T]hey are far too commonly the enemy of good software development rather than its friend.'

Deloitte found that 'redesigning our organisation to be more digital and responsive' was the number one trend in 2018 and that teams should form, change and disband quickly over time to achieve the objectives that had been set. It's important to understand, though, that taking a more agile approach isn't about taking shortcuts; it's about minimising the needless handovers and paperwork and using shorter cycles to deliver something that works. This approach will not suit everything a culture does, and will work for some things better than others.

Ultimately, however, its success—like that of just about everything else—relies on the behaviours of people, from those commissioning the work to those undertaking it. It requires that individuals are trusted to take what they judge to be the best approach to deliver a piece of work within the time, cost and quality guidelines they have been set.

Quality can never be compromised, but through regular interaction and collaboration and by taking on board ideas that contribute to the outcomes, it can be continually improved to deliver in a way that enhances the experience for all and removes the barriers to getting things done.

An agile approach to delivery isn't suitable in all cases. It's important to recognise that this is true of every process. There are some things that need to happen in a particular way at a particular time, but everything else should be continually challenged.

UNLOCK PARALYSIS WITH ANALYSIS AND ACTION

For me, the critical role that business process analysts play is in determining what's no longer needed or what could be done better. They aren't used to 'pretty' things up in Microsoft Visio or draw elaborate swim lanes in which everyone drowns.

They should be fully conversant with all kinds of process approaches and be able to adapt delivery of products and services to them. They should be creative, with excellent listening and problem-solving skills, and be able to turn bumpy approaches into smooth pathways.

Too much process goes untouched in cultures because of organisational paralysis and a fear of change at a senior management level. They become blinded by traditional ways of doing things and don't trust the good people they've hired and promoted to find a better way.

That is, until they hear of a competitor implementing 'new ways of working' and immediately decide to follow suit. What's interesting about these initiatives is that they are almost always implemented in a traditional way, thus undermining the very essence of what they're trying to do!

Of course, what's required with new ways of working is new ways of behaving, which is what holds back cultural evolution time and again. Some members of senior management particularly will be uncomfortable with losing the safety blanket of a 100-page document, consultation of 50 people or a place in a decision-making process. But in an ever-evolving culture, this has to happen.

A good analyst can spot the bottlenecks, knots and inefficiencies in a process, but only through the actions and behaviours of those involved in it can it change. Where complex problems exist, then an approach such as systems thinking can be applied to break them down.

The systems thinking approach was developed in 1956 by Professor Jay Forrester and his team at MIT's Sloan School of Management. It looks at how all processes across the culture interconnect and interrelate and is especially popular in the research sector. It uses simulation, models and graphs and, crucially, looks at behaviour over time to emulate the effects of management decisions on the system.

What I like about systems thinking is that it continually looks for inaccuracies in a cultural process system and ensures that everyone working within it constantly challenges their biases and preconceived ideas of the 'way things should work'. They ask themselves, 'Is this a problem or a symptom?'

As a culture, you should always be looking to address the symptoms in order to eradicate the problems. Using systems thinking you observe the outputs being created by the process inputs, which are a series of interconnected parts, and use feedback loops to adjust the system as you go, looking for inaccuracies or barriers to getting things done.

Every working culture requires an element of certainty in the way it gets things done. Ultimately, however, only through trusting and empowering its people to find the right way to do things can it hope to reduce complexity and red tape, increase certainty of delivery and improve the customer experience.

As Brian Chesky, founder and CEO of Airbnb, says, 'The stronger a culture, the less corporate process it requires.'

CASE STUDY: DBS

DBS, with headquarters in Singapore, is the largest bank in South-East Asia. It has one of the highest credit ratings and was rated Safest Bank of the Year six years running. In 2018 it was named by *Global Finance* as Bank of the Year.

Many of the accolades it continues to receive are a result of the fact that it continually assesses its processes and look for better ways to do things. It wasn't always that way.

In 2009 they were considered one of the worst banks. Chief Data and Transformation Officer Paul Cobban joked in an interview that on his first day a taxi driver told him that DBS stood for 'Damn Bloody Slow'! That was at the start of a program that would completely transform the bank.

They agreed on a new set of core values and set about finding ways to eliminate wasted customer time. Crucial to this was changing the decision-making process. Before the start of the program, all decisions had to be confirmed by email, which consistently caused delays. So Cobban instituted weekly meetings in which people could present their ideas in person and get an immediate decision.

They were the first bank in Singapore to launch a mobile banking wallet and the first in India to launch a mobile-only bank. They also created the first online service in Asia for opening accounts easily. They changed call centre scripts to better understand and help their customers and put the emphasis on redesigning the customer experience.

All told, they took out over 250 million wasted customer hours, and a year later they had the best customer satisfaction scores in Singapore.

KEY POINTS

- Create enough process so people understand the critical elements, and no more.

- New ways of working require a mindset and behaviour shift, not a process one.

- Increased trust leads to less bureaucracy.

ACTION YOU CAN TAKE

- Reduce the documentation you use to justify things to yourself.

- Simplify the language used in processes and documents.

- Find ways to reduce the time it takes to get something approved; this will require behaviour change for some.

- Set expectations around quality, time and cost, then trust staff to find the best way to do the work.

- For long-term growth, focus on new ways of behaving, not new ways of working.

SYSTEMS & TOOLS

In my 30 years of employment I have seen a fair few management systems. Either they were a response to the fact that things weren't working as they should, or someone else (usually a competitor) was doing it, and we felt like we had to keep up. The three I remember best are ISO 9000, Six Sigma and Lean.

Quality management standards system ISO 9000 (ISO = International Organisation for Standardisation) was revised in the year 2000, and everything we did had to be rewritten in as many words as possible in order to meet the requirements. I remember it as a laborious exercise driven by a highly analytical person who did nothing to gain buy-in for its adoption at any level, which led to the whole activity petering out. Which in hindsight was a shame as some of the principles were sound, especially in the 2015 revision, which is much more focused on culture (rather than process).

Then it was Six Sigma. Made famous by Jack Welch at GE in the 1990s, the Six Sigma approach was actually developed in 1980 by Motorola engineer Bill Smith, who trademarked it in 1993. According to Wikipedia, 'A six sigma process is one in which 99.99966% of all opportunities to produce some feature of a part are statistically expected to be free of defects.'

Essentially, Six Sigma was about continually improving process to make it more predictable and repeatable, and each project we undertook had a specific measurable value target around productivity, cost or time that we had to hit. Strong decision making is key to Six Sigma projects and it requires a certain kind of management — which we lacked, if I'm honest.

What most people got excited about, though, was the belts. There are five belts; white, yellow, green, black and master black. Like most systems, in the organisation that I worked in it became about the attainment of the belt rather than the application of the method.

Jeff Bezos at Amazon is big on Six Sigma and has talked about it frequently in interviews. In 2007 he talked about the organisation's focus on defect reduction and execution, which he had to learn about. Of Six Sigma he said,

> I have the right instincts to be an acceptable operator, but I didn't have the tools to create repeatable processes and to know where those processes made sense ... [E]xecution focus is a big factor, and you can see it in our financial metrics over the past ten years.

The Lean approach was made famous by Toyota in the 1950s and focuses on minimising waste within a production system without losing any productive working time. Toyota didn't actually use the term *lean* in their TPS (Toyota Production System). It was introduced by James P. Womack, Daniel T. Jones and Daniel Roos in their 1991 book, *The Machine That Changed the World*, which centred on an MIT study on the future of the automobile.

What has made the lean approach so incredibly successful for Toyota is that the culture has evolved over the past six decades to specifically look for ways to eliminate waste when building products and to do so in a way that values people. The framework (as they call it) is built on two main pillars:

1. **Just-in-time manufacturing.** Developed by Kiichiro Toyoda, the founder of Toyota Motor Corporation, it means 'making only what is needed, when it is needed and in the amount needed'. I've tried to apply this system at home with the breakfast cereal, but to no avail. I still end up rinsing cornflakes out of the sink.

2. **Jikoda.** This Japanese word signifies 'automation with a human touch', which means building quality into a process rather than inspecting for it at the end of the process. Everyone in the organisation has the authority to stop a process and fix it immediately, rather than wait until the end. Most organisations would see this as a waste, but Toyota are proof that it can work.

Detail-focused, analytical senior managers love to obsess about management systems, and Toyota and Amazon are proof that when applied in the right way they can work. However, like every method, they need to be accompanied by a healthy dose of EQ; otherwise people tend to feel like they're working in a dictatorship, with one person furiously trying to get people to understand their doctrine for success. As you can tell, my experiences weren't good ones!

TECHNOLOGY CAN BE A GAME CHANGER

One thing that every culture needs to consider is how it uses technology to support its people, and internal operations and digital transformation projects are popping up all over the world to do just that.

One of the biggest mistakes of digital transformation projects, though, is that they make the change about the implementation of technology rather than the evolution of culture. Implementing a new IT system creates the opportunity to help the evolution of culture but isn't responsible for it. As we've already seen, culture is so much more than technology, and vice versa.

Research by North Carolina State University reviewed in *The Wall Street Journal* in December 2018 reported that digital transformation projects were considered to be the biggest risks to organisations in 2019.

The technology that cultures have available to them has changed immeasurably over the past 10 years—from farmers using drones to monitor their cattle, to sports players wearing heart monitors, to office workers using digital tools to help them collaborate and share work progress.

Most cultures assume, incorrectly, that their people have the skills to be able to pick up new tools and applications immediately. Yet according to a Singapore Management University study in 2018, only 41 per cent of people surveyed said they had the digital skills they needed.

This is often defined as a generational thing, and it's a fact that the generation now entering the workforce have grown up with this technology. But the generational argument offers an easy out for those who don't want to apply the time and effort to learn how to use technology to add value to or track the work they do.

Digital fluency is a crucial skill for everyone within a culture today because it enables them to use the tools at their disposal to enhance their ways of working together. It's simply not acceptable for cultures not to work together to leverage the benefits that technology can provide. From task management to project management, from budget tracking to goal tracking and from inventory management to dispatch, there are tools out there to enhance almost every area of the way cultures work.

Incredibly, there are still some people who are in denial about the role technology will play in our future, who long for the 'good old days' and who marvel at the fact that kids would rather watch others play games on YouTube than play them themselves. This is the way the world is now and it needs to be embraced.

As Laszlo Bock says in *Work Rules: Insights from Inside Google That Will Transform How You Live and Lead*, 'The most talented people on the planet are increasingly physically mobile [and] increasingly connected through technology.'

Founder and Executive Chairman of the World Economic Forum, Professor Klaus Schwab, calls this 'The Fourth Industrial Revolution' in his book of the same name. It's a revolution that he sees as 'characterised by a range of new technologies that are fusing the physical, digital and biological worlds, impacting all disciplines, economies and industries, and even challenging ideas about what it means to be human'. And the success (or otherwise) of this revolution, he says, will be determined by each person's ability to use it to work together regardless of location, sector or task. It's not going to be easy, but then nothing worthwhile ever is.

Information Technology (IT) departments have a responsibility to make it simple to understand and easy to use (which has often been lacking). How many productive hours are still lost while PCs update first thing in the morning or you try to decode what someone is telling you in order to get an application working again?

Organisations have a shocking record of IT project delivery (see under 'Process & compliance') and change management (see 'Making culture stick'). If technology is to be employed for good within a culture, then IT need to get their act together and *show* others how to do it, not just tell them.

I worked in IT for the best part of 15 years and saw first-hand some of the behaviours that hold cultures back, and the reticence to challenge them. There has also been the rise of what is called Shadow IT, which essentially means other people within an organisation doing technology themselves because they don't trust their IT department to do it.

As soon as this happens you have a cultural problem. Some people see Shadow IT as a good thing, in holding IT to its word. It's not; rather, it's a cultural nightmare. IT's role is to work with other areas of the organisation and support the culture in its adoption and use of technology, and find new ways for it to be productive and collaborative. They need to be experts at this (and the communication that comes with it), or they should be moved on.

Of particular importance are the decisions made when the strategy is being built and the projects are being delivered. There are still too many meetings that produce too little action. People are reticent to make a call on which way to go, and before you know it a project has attracted more scope than it has time or money for, or else it has been superseded by something flashier and newer.

The agile approach to delivery is trying to address this issue by creating small, self-motivating teams that deliver value more quickly and frequently to customers; however, this approach is just part of the toolkit for successful delivery, not all of it. Once the right approach is determined, a decision must be made and the culture must stick to it.

Decision making is not something that all cultures are great at. Change can often feel like walking up a staircase at Hogwarts. Your world can change at any moment and you only have a split second to decide what to do.

In a McKinsey podcast in January 2018, senior partner Aaron de Smet identified four types of decisions that people have to make within a working culture:

1. **Big bet.** These are the large, transformational decisions. It could be a merger or acquisition, stop/go on a big project or a response to a major event. Every year there are likely to be one to three decisions like this that have a big impact on the organisation

2. **Cross-functional.** Consultation plays a part here as many stakeholders or different parts of the culture may be involved, and each of these smaller decisions can impact on a much larger one.

3. **Delegated.** The person who has the most knowledge is trusted to make the right call on behalf of the culture. They may seek the perspectives or opinions of others, but ultimately they will make the call.

4. **Ad-hoc.** These are small, contained decisions that happen frequently. They require neither time nor consultation and can be made by whoever is best informed at that time.

Decisions, of course, belong to all parts of a culture and once made they should be committed to. Failed technology projects often have nothing at all to do with the functionality of the thing being implemented and everything to do with the fact that the commitment wasn't made to use it consistently across the culture. Without commitment and consistent application, value will never be achieved and the culture will stagnate.

A central tool in almost all cultures is email.

THE EMAIL PROBLEM

At work today there's a very good chance—particularly in an office environment—that people are getting too many emails.

According to Atlassian's 'You Waste a Lot of Time at Work' survey, people receive on average more than 300 business emails a week and check their email 36 times an hour.

Research reported by Adam Alter in his book *Irresistible: The rise of addictive technology and the business of keeping us hooked* found that 70 per cent of office emails are read within six seconds of arrival!

In cultures where meetings are king, these emails are often checked when attention should be being paid elsewhere. Alter also found that people spend an average of three hours a day on their phones; before the smartphone era it was 18 minutes.

The definitive survey on email statistics (if that's your thing) is produced every year by the Radicati Group. In their most recent survey they reported, 'The total number of business and consumer emails sent and received per day will exceed 293 billion in 2019, and is forecast to grow to over 347 billion by year-end 2023.' Hands up if it feels like you already receive 347 billion every week? Okay, put your hands down, I've made my point.

If your culture is email heavy, then you need to understand one thing: everyone is part of the problem. If everyone who sent emails stopped sending most of them, then far fewer would be arriving in people's inboxes, storage wouldn't cost so much, privacy breaches would be reduced, people would get their evenings and weekends back (more on that in a minute), and they'd have more time to do the job they're actually paid to do.

A key mistake that most cultures make is in not setting expectations with regard to email when someone new joins the organisation. So they copy what they see others doing, and before you know it they're checking their phone every six seconds.

Then there is the expectation that email will be checked outside working hours during the week and at the weekend. This 'always on' mindset is bad for so many reasons, not least the mental health of those working in the culture.

A study on electronic communications released by Virginia Tech University in August 2018 found, 'The mere expectations of availability increase strain for employees and their significant others—even when employees do not engage in actual work during nonwork time.' So even the expectation of work (not the work itself) is bad for the employee *and* their family.

The French government recognised this in January 2017 when it passed a law making it a legal requirement for employers with over 50 employees to set out the hours when staff are required to send or answer emails. Called the 'right to disconnect' law, it's a good move, as it ensures that expectations around out-of-office email are clear. This is something that can be copied by cultures everywhere without the need for legislation.

A resource I recommend is the Email Charter (now reproduced by Nenad Maljković on his *Medium* blog). It's something that's worth adopting if your organisation has an email problem.

The Email Charter was developed by TED curator Chris Anderson and TED scribe Jane Wulf in 2011, since which more than 100 people have further contributed to it to make it what it is today. The Charter identifies 10 'rules to reverse the email spiral':

1. **Respect recipients' time.** Think about the amount of time people will need to spend reading your email.

2. **Short or slow is not rude.** Don't worry if you don't receive an immediate reply or it's not the detailed response you were expecting.

3. **Celebrate clarity.** Use a subject line that captures the topic and maybe includes what's expected (e.g. FOR INFO or ACTION).

4. **Quash open-ended questions.** Ask easy-to-answer questions, not ambiguous, lazy 'Thoughts?'-type questions.

5. **Slash surplus CC's.** This is my personal favourite because I hate CC's. They're lazy and used to cover your back. And when someone Replies All, the problem is compounded.

6. **Tighten the thread.** Conversations move on, so before replying delete any earlier parts of the thread that are no longer relevant.

7. **Attack attachments.** Don't attach complicated images or logos to emails.

8. **Give these gifts: EOM (end of message) or NNTR (no need to reply).** If your email can be said in five words, then add either or both these in the subject line.

9. **Cut countless responses.** Think carefully about the emails you need to reply to and those that simply waste your time (e.g. 'Thanks for your note!').

10. **Disconnect.** Spending less time on email will mean you receive less email!

There are now a plethora of collaboration tools that cut down on the need for email. Slack is the market leader, but many others have followed, such as the recently launched Microsoft Teams. This is an example of technology trumping technology, if it's used in the right way. If employees are spending as much time messaging on Slack as they were on email, then they've simply shifted the problem to another system!

CASE STUDY: LaSalle Network

LaSalle Network is a staffing, recruitment and culture company based in Chicago. Five years ago, Founder and CEO Tom Gimbal found that a small number of miscommunications via email could often lead to hours of anxiety for staff, so they decided to introduce an email-free workday.

They do it every three months, and there's no pattern to it (each time it falls on a different weekday). During the day itself, no email may be checked between 8 am and 5 pm, with two 20-minute breaks to check for and respond to emergencies only.

So everyone knows what's going on, they set an out-of-office message and ask people to call instead. The initiative has been hugely successful and as a business they've realised the following values:

- **Speed.** When they want to get in touch with a client, they've learned that phoning is quicker. And rather than emailing their co-workers, they pop over for a chat.

- **Empathy.** More time improves communication and leads to greater empathy.

- **Creativity.** Doing things 'live' rather than consulting over email has led to different ideas coming to the fore.

- **Encourages 'CBE'.** 'Call Before Email' is something they now practise every day.

- **Greater energy.** The energy on no-email days is different from that on other days, with more people walking, talking and spending time on the phone.

KEY POINTS

- If you're using a management system, make sure everyone understands their role within it.

- Technology can improve the way you do things, if used in the right way.

- Draw up a charter for email use, and make sure everyone follows it.

ACTION YOU CAN TAKE

There are many things that people can do to reduce the number of emails they receive. Creating communities to try a few of these out and report back to each other on their effectiveness will increase the chances of these initiatives working. Here are a few that have proved useful:

- Complete a task before checking email.

- Don't check email before you arrive in the office or after you leave.

- If you have a work phone, lock it in an office drawer (unless you're on call).

- Uninstall the email app from your phone. I did this regularly and highly recommend it. If people need you they'll phone, trust me.

- Turn off notifications to prevent distraction.

- Open your email on your laptop or PC only twice a day (say, at 10 am and 2 pm). A boss of mine who did this regularly had a zero inbox and enjoyed great face-to-face discussions with people.

- Set yourself a daily email limit and don't go over it.

- Set an email-free day once a month.

Finally, a word of advice from entrepreneur, Gary Vaynerchuk: 'Train yourself to do a little bit more in each hour than you normally would.'

WORKING ENVIRONMENT

Okay, let's start with a fact. Open-plan offices, as a single catch-all mechanism to improve collaboration between team members, don't work.

I'm sorry if you've just spent thousands of dollars on going down that path, but you shouldn't have jumped on the bandwagon before doing some research. Had you done so you'd have found that the initiative you hoped would 'pull down the barriers', get people away from their desks and increase face-to-face collaboration time actually reduces it by 73 per cent, according to a recent survey of Fortune 500 companies. Not only that, but one study from Harvard University found that email went up by 67 per cent and the use of messaging tools by 75 per cent.

Offices where people have a desk they call their own are on the decline. As reported in *The Wall Street Journal*, a privately conducted survey of 138 employers in the US found that by 2021, 52 per cent—slightly more than half—plan to replace 'reserved' desks with 'first-come, first-served desks, plus additional workspaces with names like huddle rooms and touchdown spaces'.

While these workspaces work for some, they most definitely don't work for others. In the rush for greater collaboration, cultures are undermining concentration and productivity by creating spaces that suit one personality type over another.

It was always thus. For decades leaders of organisations around the world have strived to create the 'perfect' environment in which all workers within a culture can do their best work. And from schools to skyscrapers the same mistakes are made as they assume either that everyone wants to work in one way or that they can readily be persuaded to change to working another way.

Frederick Winslow Taylor was the first person to have a crack at it back in the early 1900s. He believed that simply making people work harder wasn't as important as improving the way people were able to do their work. He outlined his ideas in his 1911 monograph *The Principles of Scientific Management*.

In it he proposed four principles, which formed the core of what became known as 'Taylorism':

1. Replace the practice of common sense or rule of thumb, whereby workers got to decide for themselves, based on experience, the right way to do something, with a 'scientific' method that would determine the most efficient way to perform a task.

2. Rather than giving any work to any person, assign people to jobs based on their motivation and train them to do them better.

3. Monitor and supervise their work to make sure they work as efficiently as they can.

4. Assign planning and training work to managers so workers can get on with the tasks at hand.

In short, he tried to create a system according to which there was one optimal way of doing any task. Managers did the planning and workers did the work. It was a highly structured and efficient way of getting work done. And for lots of companies it worked. The Ford Motor Company provided the most famous case study. Henry Ford had Taylor study everything about the production line and in 1913 an entirely new assembly line was built at Highland Park.

In a matter of years — and with Taylor's help — Ford had reduced the time it took to create a Model T to 93 minutes, which allowed them to lower the price from \$825 to \$575. This gave Ford a whopping 48 per cent of the auto market at that time. He raised staff wages and by the end of 1924 he'd sold 10 million cars.

But people aren't cars, and while Taylorism certainly helped to streamline assembly-line processes, it just wasn't suitable for day-to-day office life. So in 1964 along came designer Robert Propst with his 'Action Office' (which, to be clear, wasn't where Action Man worked). The aim of the Action Office was to provide staff with a quiet, creative space that could be moved and reconfigured as required — a 'just for you' space, if you will, in which a person could do their best work.

Much to his dismay, Propst's utopian conception of the creative space was reimagined as the space-saving cubicle popularised by the Herman Miller Company.

The Gen-X movie that brought the folly of the cubicle as a creative space out into the open is Mike Judge's masterpiece *Office Space*. In the movie, computer programmer Peter Gibbons, brilliantly played by Ron Livingston, uses his cubicle to hide from his boss and co-workers.

In one scene he says, 'Human beings were not meant to sit in little cubicles staring at computer screens all day, filling out useless forms and listening to eight different bosses drone on about mission statements.'

He was speaking for a generation of frustrated office workers, and in the early 2000s we started to see the walls come tumbling down. But what does Newton's third law say? For every action there is an equal and opposite reaction. If cubicles killed creativity and collaboration, it's only natural to assume that taking the walls down encourages it, right? Er, no.

Unsurprisingly, research shows that when people aren't able to focus on a task without interruption or distraction, it undermines the quality of their work. Also, when they can't concentrate they communicate less. So it's a lose–lose scenario for everyone.

If a quiet work environment isn't provided, some employees will simply create one by putting on headphones to block out the distracting noise, replacing it with motivational noise. You see this approach everywhere. From operating theatres, to sporting arenas with athletes preparing themselves for their event, to IT departments where banks of people sit in silence with big cans on the sides of their heads.

General Stanley McChrystal writes in *Team of Teams*, 'How we organize physical space says a lot about how we think people behave; but how people behave is often a by-product of how we set up physical space.' Working environments should never alienate the people who work in them. Rather, they should be a haven for behaviour that inspires productive work, while recognising that different personalities like to work in different ways.

I've long been an advocate of personality-based working, in which organisations create a variety of workspaces that suit different preferences and people can choose which one best allows them—at any given moment of their day—to be the most productive version of themselves. This means a combination of private, quiet, group and social spaces that can be used by anyone at any time. If you want a permanent desk, no problem. If you want to hot desk, likewise. Just don't force a personality into a space that won't enable them to be productive.

Most adults know exactly what they need to do their best work; it's up to the organisation to provide for these needs. Providing a range of spaces in this way plays to the strengths of the staff and ensures that headphones aren't required to 'block out culture'.

Richard Sheridan talks about this in his book *Joy Inc.*:

> If everyone is allowed to close his or her door or block out the world with earbuds the chances of overhearing others just won't occur. Space and noise play a huge factor in creating the opportunity for allowing teamwork to work its magic.

Menlo Innovations have put time and effort into creating spaces that suit the individuals who work there and to create environments where you're able to step out of these and work closely with others.

And yes, ping pong tables, foosball tables and bean bags are all included in these areas, but they are peripheral to the work or conversations taking place there.

Thankfully the era of dreary, unimaginative, one-size-fits-all workspaces is coming to an end, and forward-thinking organisations are putting the requirements of their staff at the forefront of design and breathing new life into offices to demonstrate what can be achieved.

Mozilla use a personality-based approach to their work environments and have four types of space:

1. collaborative
2. social
3. focus
4. private.

Spotify's new office in Stockholm brilliantly reflects the company itself while providing an invigorating space for staff to work in. It includes:

- a recording studio
- a stage for live performances
- a board game zone

- a bar

- a karaoke room

- games and craft areas.

These won't sound like traditional work spaces, and that's because they're not! They are spaces to talk, share ideas, collaborate and re-energise. Of course there are still desks (standing and sitting) where people can use a laptop and whiteboards for groups, but the whole environment is stimulating.

The same is true of the new Google office in London, which boasts a gym, library, climbing wall and roof garden, to name just a few of the fringe benefits that make it such a desirable place to work.

I know what you're thinking. What if you don't have the money for this or management with the courage or mindset to think creatively about office layout? Well, you can do what my teams and I often did — you can change it yourself.

Oh, there'll be people in Facilities Management (particularly) who'll tell you that what you want to do can't be done, and line managers who'll insist there's no budget for it and you'll have to make do. Ignore these people! In a highly emotionally intelligent way, of course.

Bring in screwdrivers to raise or lower partitions to create spaces for individuals. Find whiteboards and tables that people aren't using and put them in your space. Use windows as whiteboards (using the right pens, obviously!), stick butchers paper to the wall to create Kanban boards or similar visual tools, and (my favourite) book a meeting room for a year and call it the library. This is the one almost everyone will tell you that you can't do, but I've done it many times, so I promise it works.

It helps if, as part of your culture work, you can cut down on the number of meetings you have, because that way it won't be booked out nearly as much.

So you have a library. It's well lit and you fill it with textbooks. No headphones or music is allowed and you can't personalise a space in there. Food, drink or talking aren't allowed either. There are other social spaces (the kitchen usually) where you can do those things.

Some fear that if you create a library people will stay in there all day and never come out. In my experience this almost never happens. In one company, such was its popularity for getting quiet, focused work completed that we ended up creating a second library in another building.

The same applies to classrooms, although space is more limited. Again, what types of personalities do you need to cater for? How do they work best? What space can be given up to large group activity, small group activity and focused work?

Does the furniture have wheels to enable you to rearrange it? Do you have partitions you can use when you need to? Is there an array of creative tools always on hand so students can be creative without leaving the room?

I never conformed to the 'use what you're given' principle when it came to workspace. Early on I always discussed with the team how we would set it up to ensure that everyone had a mix of personal and group space, and anything that didn't work was changed.

FLEXIBLE WORKING ARRANGEMENTS

In the late 1990s and early 2000s working from home became a thing.

Actually it had been a thing for a while before then, but with the implementation of new technologies that allowed people to replicate their offices at home, the demand for 'working from home' days and more flexible working arrangements increased. And having access to the right technology is crucial to bridging the gap between office and home.

In stagnant and combatant cultures there is still deep scepticism about the need to work from home, especially when the statistics show that teams that are co-located are more effective.

Still, the advantages of flexible working are there for all to see, including:

- cost savings (in both travel and real estate)
- less stress
- fewer distractions (if you prefer a quieter environment)
- better health (with less time spent on sedentary, stressful commuting)
- better work–life balance.

There are some disadvantages too, though, and as an extrovert who runs his own practice I see lots of these. They include:

- isolation (you're no longer interacting directly with people every day)
- distractions (home is more comfortable and it's easy to waste time 'popping the washing on')
- being always on (working at home, surrounded by distractions, requires discipline)
- strain on relationships (through always being on and not separating work and family time).

For workers with children or dependents, flexible working can help to ensure that a balance is maintained and that both family and work are attended to. Indeed, in my experience, allowing staff to design their own week builds loyalty and generates a more productive and trusting environment.

Trust is critical in making working from home viable, as is the skill of being able to set expectations well. And the latter is sadly lacking in most organisations. Organisations like to send their staff on communications skills courses, but in my experience over the past few years, knowing how to set expectations is one of the top three skills required when working with different cultures.

Only when expectations are set—around what's required, to what quality and by when—can productivity be measured at the end of the week. This in turn builds trust, which increases productivity and loyalty. Similarly, when expectations aren't met, then an empathetic conversation can be held around what specifically went wrong.

In the early days of flexible working I had two people who worked from home two to three days a week. Given all the travel involved and the fact that we had to be in different cities at different times of the week, it made no sense for us all to come into the office every day.

At the start the arrangement didn't work. I frequently felt sceptical about how the working-from-home time was being used, and often my suspicions got the better of me. I felt that time was being wasted. The root of the problem, though, was the fact that I hadn't set expectations well. I didn't fully trust one team member, who was never able to provide me with what I was looking for. Imagine that!

Fortunately I could talk it over with my boss, who told me to use my one-on-ones at the start of the week to set expectations, ensuring that each member understood them, then let them get on with it. This made it easy for me to check in with that person during the week to ensure they were on track and provide positive and constuctive feedback as appropriate.

After about four weeks the issue was resolved and work became very much a thing we did, not a place we went. But in getting there, new routines had to be developed. People still had to get dressed for work in the morning, even if they weren't heading into the office. The technology had to work and you had to be available for calls at certain times of the day. Flexible working doesn't mean a lack of discipline.

In some organisations that have fully embraced flexible working it has become a core part of their culture. For example, more than 80 per cent of Intel's staff work flexibly. Many others are struggling with it, however. Within weeks of being appointed as CEO of Yahoo in 2013, Marissa Mayer announced she was putting an end to working from home. 'To become the absolute best place to work,' she said, 'communication and collaboration will be important, so we need to be working side-by-side. That is why it is critical that we are all present in our offices.'

'Marissa felt like it was the right thing to do for Yahoo at this time,' explained a PR spokesperson the next day, and of course that was her prerogative. However, the message it sent to staff, who weren't slow in registering their views, was that they weren't trusted, which is not the message you want to send as a new CEO looking to reinvigorate an organisation. It was a move backward, when everyone else was moving forward.

California-based digital marketing agency Wpromote have almost 400 people on their payroll and their CEO, Mike Mothner, knows what it takes to create a great culture. They encourage and trust all of their employees to work from home. Alternatively they can bring elements of home into the office—which is, for instance, a dog-friendly space.

As the gig economy continues to grow, so will flexible working arrangements, with short-term assignments and independent contractors becoming more prevalent over the next 10 years. Many new start-ups are making the decision not to buy office space, but instead are looking to property organisations such as We:Work to provide them with an environment and the technology that are fit for purpose without the need for a long-term investment in real estate.

Ultimately, when it comes to creating workspaces for the culture you want, they need to be personal and flexible, providing different spaces for focus, interaction, consultation and socialisation. It must consider the needs of projects and teams, and provide technology and creative tools that blend seamlessly into the working day.

What is important isn't where someone is but what they produce. If they need to be in an office to do what's needed, then so be it; otherwise, if expectations are set and managed well, the work can be done in their own space at their own pace.

CASE STUDY: KHDA

The Knowledge and Human Development Authority (KHDA), the education authority of Dubai, in the United Arab Emirates, is on a mission to transform the way people think about education.

As well as creating networks of teams with no hierarchy, sharing work on the basis of talent and interests, and providing a program of activities to help staff become fitter and healthier, they encourage their people to design their own workspace.

Only a few walled offices remain for more personal meetings. Employees have been given full responsibility for creating the kinds of spaces they need both to build an environment where they can do their best work and to work together most effectively.

KEY POINTS

- As a single mechanism to improve collaboration, open-plan offices don't work.

- A variety of spaces should be created so different personality types can choose the environment in which they can do their best work.

- Flexible working arrangements are highly effective provided high levels of trust exist.

ACTION YOU CAN TAKE

When creating spaces for people to do their best work, don't get lazy and simply copy what others have done. Take the time to consider the type of work you do, the personalities of your people and the requirements of the culture and subcultures. Ensure that it's easy to make changes and that there are high levels of trust.

If your working environment doesn't provide a quiet space in which introverts can work, then think about what you can do to create one. Creating a 'library' is one option, but quiet corners or spaces should be easy to provide.

Larger collaboration spaces are good for more extroverted activity, but they can also be broken up into smaller group areas for more targeted work. Staff should never feel restricted by the spaces in which they work.

PILLAR 6
INNOVATION

Just as it's true that culture belongs to everyone, it's also true that innovation is everyone's job.

If you've been reading this book in sequential order and have most of the cultural things I've outlined in place already, then there's a good chance that new and better ways of doing things will just happen without prompting or reminding people that innovation is important. They'll understand that and make it a priority.

In these kinds of cultures senior people encourage innovation and practise it themselves. After all, the same people expect employees to keep their products or services to customers continually fit for purpose for the environment in which they operate. Whether it's a hairdressing salon offering the latest cut or a lawnmower using the latest technology, if innovation doesn't occur naturally, then cultures run the risk of being overtaken or forgotten altogether.

There's a generation of people who will never understand the concept of taking a completed roll of photographic film to a photo store and the excitement of picking up 24, 36 or 48 photos in a paper wallet a week later. And the next Kodak—the most famous example of an organisation that failed to innovate—is just around the corner. Analysts regularly debate who this might be.

One company it won't be is Amazon, who place great emphasis on innovation across their business. One of their leadership principles is: 'Invent and Simplify. Leaders expect and require innovation and invention from their teams and always find ways to simplify. They are externally aware, look for new ideas from everywhere, and are not limited by "not invented here".'

The 'not invented here' mindset often holds people back. They remain too narrowly focused on what the organisation has 'traditionally' done, rather than on new possibilities. For those with fixed mindsets, daily challenges can be solved only by conventional means, yet 'challenge and finding the right level of it' is one of the key ways to create a culture of innovation, according to Australian author and creativity guru Amantha Imber.

Innovation is rarely easy, which is why few cultures make it a core tenet of what they do. Instead they resort to quick-fix attempts at it. In a tongue-in-cheek 2018 blog, author Sarah Cooper listed 12 such short cuts. These include attending innovation events, hiring a Chief Innovation Officer and creating an innovation lab! Actually, I'm not against these spaces, but I am against the notion that only certain people, working in certain areas, will generate the ideas. Innovation ideas can be conceived by anyone, given the right conditions and encouragement.

THE CONDITIONS FOR INNOVATION

For innovation to become a true pillar of your culture there are many hurdles that need to be overcome. An innovation leaders survey of 270 business leaders in July 2018 listed the top five obstacles to innovation at large companies as:

a. politics/turf wars (cited by 55 per cent of respondents)

b. cultural issues (45 per cent)

c. inability to act (42 per cent)

d. lack of budget (41 per cent)

e. lack of strategy/vision (36 per cent).

All these obstacles must be addressed to make innovation a thing that gets done, not talked about.

What innovation requires most of all is senior management support, time and an understanding that things won't always work.

The average working day for most people in offices is swamped by endless meetings and interactions that add little value to their days or to the outcomes the organisation seeks. That's not to say that every innovation creates value. But as I will soon discuss, only through failure can we ever hope to succeed.

Not all innovation is good, despite what you might be told in flashy marketing launches.

Juicero was launched in the US in 2017 to much fanfare (especially by *The New York Times*). Having received US$120 million in venture capital funding from organisations such as Alphabet and Kleiner Perkins Caulfield and Byers, it went into production with a US$700 juicer with associated pouches for people to 'press their own juice'.

And then a video from Bloomberg that went viral showed that you didn't need the Juicero machine to get the juice out of the pouches—you could just squeeze it out with your hands. And just like that the idea and the business died.

In this case it was an interesting enough idea, but it should never have made it to market.

The willingness of senior executives within cultures to free up time for their people to work on different things (that might or might not produce results), to take risks and commit to seeing them through, has to be high. Innovation must be taken seriously and as a core business activity.

It's hard for some to let go of tradition. Some managers still insist on people being seen at their desks and sticking to more conventionally productive work. Had the management at 3M done that, the Post-it note would never have been born. Similarly with AdWords over at Google. Both are examples of ideas that were created then further developed using time provided for innovation.

IT STARTS AT THE TOP

In low-innovation cultures those in senior positions have to be the enablers of innovation. Some people within the culture with a tendency to grow bored or frustrated with the current modus operandi are likely to go looking for innovation. Everyone else will look for permission or encouragement to do so from those in higher authority.

The Deloitte Capital Trends Report in 2017 observed, 'High performing organisations focus on building a new leadership mindset that rewards innovation, experimentation, learning and customer-centric design-thinking.' A McKinsey paper of the same year, 'Culture for a Digital Age', stated, 'Executives themselves [must] act boldly once they have decided on a specific digital play.' And of course it doesn't need to be a digital play; it can be anything at all related to improving the outcomes for the organisation.

In 2009 researchers Christensen, Dyer and Gregorsen studied 3000 executives over six years to better understand what characteristics the most innovative leaders had. They found three things:

1. Senior execs of most innovative companies were innovators themselves.

2. These leaders displayed 50 per cent more discovery skills than the less innovate companies.

3. The innovative success of an organisation is largely determined by senior execs leading by example.

According to the Global Innovation Index in 2018, the energy sector is one area that will require innovation given that some consumption projections estimate that as a planet we'll need 30 per cent more energy in 2040 than we need today.

The battery farm that Tesla stood up in Southern Australia in less than a month in 2017 is a great example of innovation. Was it a challenge? Yes. Did it have senior management/political commitment? Eventually. (It took the intervention of Atlassian co-founder Mike Cannon-Brookes to gain full support.) Is it now a model that could be replicated elsewhere in the world? Absolutely.

And would any of this be possible if Elon Musk didn't lead by example? No.

He's a polarising figure is Elon. At the time of writing, the US SEC (Securities and Exchange Commission) is seeking to have him charged for influencing the stock market through his tweets. Yet it's hard to challenge the fact that he's currently one of the world's greatest innovators. True, his people skills (like those of Steve Jobs) leave a little to be desired, and you need high levels of resilience to work for one of his organisations. Still, from electric cars to hyper loop trains via battery farms, he's not a person who's attached to 'not invented here'.

In a biography by Ashlee Vance, one employee was asked about his views on how Musk responded to fixed mindset people who were stuck on the current ways things are done. He replied,

> We have meetings and take bets on who is going to get bloody and bruised. If you told him that you made a particular choice because 'it was the standard way things had always been done' he'd kick you out [and] say 'I never want to hear that phrase again.'

If innovation is important, then 'standard ways of doing things' must be constantly questioned.

Back to the Christensen, Dyer and Gregorsen study of 2009. They found that innovative senior managers spent 50 per cent more time on five discovery activities. Here I present these activities with actionable things that can be done in each to become the kind of person who supports innovation regardless of role:

1. **Associating.** You are able to connect different pieces of information from different places, often outside the organisation. This requires lots of spare-time research, for example reading blogs or listening to podcasts where you might learn something that might be relevant to a similar scenario within your culture.

2. **Questioning.** You ask questions designed to help others overcome their fixed mindset or viewpoint. The most obvious one is 'Why?', but others include 'Why not?', 'If not us, then who?', 'What if?' and 'What are the consequences of *not* doing this?' You are looking to remove any roadblocks (perceived or real) to moving an idea forward.

3. **Observing.** Innovators never stop looking and listening. They see and hear ideas everywhere. Airbnb offers a great example of this. The business was born because CEO Brian Chesky couldn't find a hotel room in San Francisco and ended up staying with a friend who had a room free. He wondered how many more people found themselves in the same boat: either they couldn't find a room or they had one they didn't use that they'd be happy to rent out. And the business was born.

4. **Experimenting.** Everyone has done this at some point in their life. Something I used to do was encourage people to swap roles or go and work in a different department. Better still, take the opportunity to work

in a different city or country. Within a work context, it's about encouraging people to try different approaches, to look at things in different ways. Remove process, use different people, ask different customers—anything fresh!

5. **Networking.** Perhaps the easiest place to start is to attend conferences, find like-minded people and share ideas about what you're doing. These might not be competitors, but people in similar roles in your city. It's something I used to do regularly, to find out what different ideas people had about building teams so I could improve what I do. I still do this today.

MAKE INNOVATION VISIBLE

Once an environment that supports innovation exists, then people need to be encouraged to use the opportunity. Finding out what others do (through networking) is a great place to start.

Deloitte Digital in Melbourne have a wall called 'The Dumbest Things', where they list ideas to be tackled. Anyone can grab one of these ideas at any time and work on it when they have time.

Pharmaceutical giant Unilever have a public innovation portal where they can post their ideas and even encourage people from outside the organisation to post theirs too.

This 'idea generation' exercise is crucial to keep innovation moving forward and to ensure that the process is as inclusive and transparent as it can be. Most cultures will require some kind of process, so individuals working on things that either don't align with the vision or could undermine other work being undertaken elsewhere are halted early.

A regular session could be held to assess these ideas for suitability, value and timing. It doesn't need to be a half-day workshop; it could be a simple stand-up meeting around a board that's been used to capture the ideas visually. The process should be a democratic one, with ideas then delegated to individuals to work on.

Better still would be to devote an entire day solely to innovation. This is what Atlassian do with their Ship-It Days. Between Thursday lunchtime and Friday lunchtime, all employees who participate (which is almost always *all* employees!) have an opportunity to come up with something and get it shipped (that is, turned into action) within 24 hours.

These sessions are high-energy events with plenty of refreshments to ensure that solutions-based thinking is continually fuelled. It's not about solving huge problems — the ideas can be incremental or purely random. For example, one idea that was put into action was simply removing some light bulbs in the San Francisco office that got too hot!

The event ends with participants giving three-minute lightning talks and a *Shark Tank*–style panel for questions and answers. The winner gets a 'token' trophy and the kudos that goes with it.

Innovation days are exciting, motivational, practical and potentially transformational. They make a point of saying 'evolution is important and we want you to be creative and curious', and they keep people and organisations fresh and interesting.

IDEO create a similar environment in which new thinking can flourish. In a 2018 blog they shared their five conditions for innovation:

1. Create a shared vision.

2. Let teams influence the space.

3. Learn how teams actually work.

4. It all starts with prototypes.

5. Codify and share what you learn.

Simple conditions that actively encourage people to not do things the way they've always done them.

Any culture can do these things. They simply have to make the time, encourage the mindset then ensure that action is taken. Great cultures never stand still. Every year the Boston Consulting Group's Most Innovative Companies list acknowledges those that have excelled at introducing and investing in new ideas, products and services.

Since 2005, BCG have been producing a report that centres on feedback from over 2000 senior business leaders and provides a ranked list of those organisations considered market leaders in innovation. From 2005 to 2017 Apple topped the list, with Alphabet/Google replacing it at number one in 2018.

With only one exception, the top 10 organisations on the 2018 list all significantly increased their research and development spend from 2017, with their primary focus being on the adoption and use of artificial intelligence in their products and services. The percentage increases in research and development were as follows:

1. Alphabet/Google (up by 19.2 per cent)

2. Amazon (40.6 per cent)

3. Apple (15.3 per cent)

4. Microsoft (8.8 per cent)

5. Samsung (15.9 per cent)

6. Netflix (23.6 per cent)

7. IBM (0.6 per cent)

8. Facebook (30.5 per cent)

9. Tesla (65.2 per cent)

10. Adidas (14.0 per cent)

Adidas was a surprise inclusion in the top 10, up from number 35 the previous year. This represents a continued commitment by the leadership team, led by its CEO Kasper Rorsted, to spending money on making their products more sustainable, which in our plastic-dominated world is something to be celebrated and encouraged. It's helped the bottom line too, with earnings before interest and tax (EBIT) up 49 per cent.

Here are three examples of their commitment to continual innovation:

- **Parley Ocean Plastic™.** Working with Parley for the Oceans, an environmental company 'defending diversity on land and sea', they are turning plastic waste into useful products and have also committed to eradicating microbeads from their products.

- **Sport Infinity.** This range of sportswear and footwear combines broken-down elements from other sports products with excess materials sourced from other industries—as the press release put it, 'so the football boots of the future could contain everything from carbon used in aircraft manufacturing to fibres of the boots that scored during the World Cup'.

- **DryDye.** The traditional dyeing process uses a lot of water, but Adidas is changing that. Its DryDye approach uses no water and 50 per cent less chemicals and energy than more established methods. By 2014 they estimated they'd already saved 100 million litres of water.

Innovation needn't require world-changing approaches (although given the state of the planet, we do need more of these!), but what it does need is leadership, time and commitment. Those cultures that don't embrace these things can expect to be left behind or to perish altogether.

CASE STUDY: Cadence Design Systems

Cadence Design Systems are an electronic design company based in San Jose, California, that manufacture semi-conductor boards and chips. Their work is crucial for the next generation of smartphones, biomedical devices and storage applications. If they were to stand still as a business they would lose competitive advantage and fall behind where consumers want their technology to take them.

CEO Lip-Bu Tan is committed to innovation and recognises that where ideas were traditionally found is not likely to be where they will be found in the future. 'As transformative trends like machine learning shape the future of electronics,' she says, 'the opportunity for Cadence to innovate and grow is immense. I am committed to fuelling a dynamic work environment where employees feel inspired and empowered to do their best work...to delight our customers with innovative products.'

She recognised the importance of different perspectives by establishing Women@Cadence, an inclusive and diverse program that fosters a culture of equality to fuel new ideas. Cadence's innovation series comprises speakers, round-table discussions and networking events, and partners with industry-leading organisations to showcase new ideas and inspire a different level of thinking.

Open to men and women alike, the program has elevated the innovation capability of its people and kept Cadence at the forefront of hardware and software development.

KEY POINTS

- Innovation occurs everywhere.
- Not all ideas are good ideas!
- Make innovation visible to create excitement and action.

ACTION YOU CAN TAKE

As a new member of staff at Atlassian you have 90 days to familiarise yourself with the organisation, staff and ways of working, then, the expectation is, change something.

Making time for creative thinking is important, but taking action is where it's at, and the idea can be anything at all. It doesn't have to be a feature change on one of their tools; it can be something functional about the office or something practical that people can do.

Every organisation can do something similar, and it sets the perfect tone for what's expected going forward. Imagine how liberating it would feel as a new employee if your previous employer was change averse and their ways of working hadn't changed in years. Suddenly you are working for an organisation that *wants* you to find something to fix, to use your knowledge, expertise and 'fresh eye' to look for opportunities to improve something that already works well. The ideas are important, but implementing them is where change happens.

CREATIVITY

If innovation is the *process* by which cultures implement or introduce new ideas, then creativity is required to generate them in the first place. Researchers de Souza, Pellissier and Monteiro argued in 2012, 'It would only become innovation if these individuals or teams worked collaboratively across the organisation to create a new collective way of doing things. Creative collaboration underpins successful organisational innovation.'

Creativity is about finding and unleashing the potential in people and their ideas. Ideas fuel creativity and are inherent in every person, regardless of role, personality or motivation. Even the most demotivated employees have ideas; often they're demotivated precisely because no one listens to them!

In order to generate ideas, thinking time needs to be allocated for this purpose. Often cultures lack creativity because they're stuck in an endless cycle of 'busy' work.

ARE YOU BUSY OR PRODUCTIVE?

One of my favourite blogs of 2018 was 'We live in the golden era of Lazy Busy' by Dominic Quartuccio, who wrote about how most people are stuck in a loop of being perpetually busy. This is something I hear every day from clients, friends and family! When you ask people how they are, they tell you they're 'busy'. When you start a conversation with someone you ask them if they're 'busy'. When individuals are being the least productive versions of themselves, they have an internal busy dialogue going on.

'Our biggest mistake,' Dominic pointed out in his blog, 'is our belief that constant action equals productivity, usefulness and/or importance.' In fact, he argues, incessant action is lazy—he terms it 'lazy busy'—and it's rife in pleasant and combatant cultures, manifested for example in:

- back-to-back meetings
- lots of people being unnecessarily CC'ed into emails
- eating lunch at their desk or during meetings
- spending time on low-value work
- not being able to say 'no'.

'People who are busy all the time are not creative,' observed the legendary physicist and mathematician Freeman Dyson. Stephen Covey wrote about this 25 years ago in his book *First Things First*. He even created an easy-to-follow model to help people to allocate their time between important and urgent work. Like most things that make sense, however, it seems his advice was largely ignored, and too many people still spend much of their work day in unproductive and lazy busy activity.

The priorities for the culture should be clear and unambiguous. Where they're not, people within the culture have a ready-made excuse for not delivering and for getting stuck in a cycle of dealing with whatever is most urgent at any given time. If you want to evolve the culture, you can't allow this to happen, because people will never make the time for creativity. It will always drop to the bottom of the list of priorities, something to be considered when things break—by which time it's too late—or else at the weekend when it's no longer possible to share the idea with a co-worker.

Collaboration is key for creativity. Just because an employee thinks they have a good idea worth implementing doesn't actually make it so. Its potential needs to be challenged, assessed and approved if it's ever to be implemented. Once you get to that point, you need an optimistic, motivated team to continually work on it to make it a reality. Putting it in the hands of a group of people who are already 'busy' means it will become just one more item on their to-do list.

I've mentioned that I'm not a fan of innovation labs as they imply that only the group of people working in the lab can come up with ideas, even though everyone has them. Having said that, they can be a useful mechanism for creating groups of cross-functional teams to be creative, share, test and implement ideas.

One of the things I like most about the agile movement is the concept of prototyping as a way of delivering value more quickly to a customer. This approach cuts out the unnecessary things within our operational process that hold back creativity, although this is only true if you put creativity in the right hands.

My favourite book on creativity is (funnily enough) *Creativity Inc.* by former president of Pixar and Walt Disney Animation Studios Ed Catmull. He notes that in the wrong hands creativity can die very quickly.

> If you give a good idea to a mediocre team they screw it up. If you give a mediocre idea to a brilliant team they will either fix it or throw it away and come up with something better. Getting the team right is the precursor to getting the ideas right.

Brilliant teams are curious, adventurous and courageous, and they need all three of these qualities in equal amounts.

CURIOUS, ADVENTUROUS AND COURAGEOUS

One of the things I've enjoyed most about being a parent has been watching the kids learn and grow. When they were younger, they would use their eyes, ears, hands and mouths fearlessly to figure stuff out. Our job as parents was to make sure that the environment was safe to do all these things and that they couldn't come to any harm.

They weren't held back by anyone's preconceived ideas about what was and wasn't 'normal'. We encouraged them to try different things and observed their reactions when the results weren't what they were expecting.

Whether it was learning to ride a bike, building things or eating different foods, it's been fascinating to watch them grow. Of course, when we're young we don't have to be told to be curious, we just are. By the time we get to work, however, our curiosity has begun to wane and we're scared to try anything new for fear of being admonished or ridiculed or of failing.

Education and development plans often focus on learning things by rote rather making time for curiosity and play. While much is down to an individual's mindset, cultures that don't make time for their staff to 'play' with ideas are missing a huge opportunity to unlock potential and build products, services and internal change that evolves the way things get done. The best way to encourage a growth mindset is to do things that stimulate rather than stymie it.

One organisation that encourages play within its culture is Lego. After a long day at the office, I used to love sitting down with one of the kids to help build a house, spaceship or something totally random out of Lego. In no time the stresses of the day would melt away as I became focused on the uniqueness of my idea, before presenting it (often to great fanfare) for critiquing. Minutes later, it would be scattered in pieces on the floor and I'd be tiptoeing around in fear that I might accidentally tread on one and be in agony for, well, hours.

Lego recognised this and created the LEGO® SERIOUS PLAY® methodology. It was developed in 1996 when two professors at the International Institute for Management Development in Switzerland, Johan Roos and Bart Victor, and then LEGO Group CEO Kjeld Kirk Kristiansen were exploring alternative strategic planning tools.

They recognised that some of the most challenging business issues could be constructed as three-dimensional models by the people in the room. They rejected the notion that external people needed to be brought in to identify the creative ideas on their behalf. People looked for ideas outside of their own area of expertise or operational group and started to look for different associations.

Thomas Møller Jeppesen, HR Director, Partnering & Operations at LEGO Group, commented, 'Play is such an important fundamental element of creativity, learning, motivation and interpersonal engagement that it seems illogical to separate it from the work environment in the way that we traditionally have.'

Having seen the methodology in action, it's fascinating to watch the evolution of people's mindsets. Often they start with an 'I'm too busy for this' narrative, but once they understand the 'rules' they quickly move to being curious. When they start to be adventurous and explore what's possible, the fun really starts.

This is where we start to see 'The Medici Effect' come into play, as explored by Frans Johannsen in his book of the same name.

The Medici family were an immensely powerful dynasty of Italian merchants and bankers who ruled the city of Florence for more than 200 years until the mid-18th century. Their family line included two Queens and four Popes, but perhaps their most profound and lasting impact on the Renaissance world was their patronage of the arts and sciences.

The Medicis used their vast wealth to support creativity, attracting to their city some of the greatest thinkers and artists of the age, Leonardo da Vinci, Michelangelo and Galileo among them. They were encouraged to discuss their ideas openly and challenge each other's thinking and action, which in turn led to two different types of adventurous thinking:

1. **Directional thinking** is about incremental improvements and refinements to what already exists. This linear thinking is generally more predictable and therefore easier to see. A good modern example of this is the self-driving car, which is a natural progression from the conventional cars of today.

2. **Intersectional thinking** doesn't follow immediately obvious pathways, making it difficult for the competition to see or predict. The outcomes of this thinking are often game changers that can then influence other intersectional thinking ideas. A good example of this is the iPod, an idea so unexpected that it caught everyone by surprise, and turned out to be the precursor to the smartphone and other devices.

The Medici Effect means bringing together people who think in different ways, encouraging them to challenge each other's thought processes, re-examine their biases and assumptions and learn to look at things in different ways.

In both ways of thinking, an idea is generated and is developed and explored further over time with a view to what is and isn't possible today and what could be possible in the future.

The more ideas are sought out, compared and interrogated, the greater the chance that the culture will stumble on something new. What's required is not luck but a sense of adventure and a readiness to challenge an idea fully before deciding on a way forward. At all stages what's needed is the courage to see the idea through from inception to implementation.

One of the reasons that British innovation company Dyson is so successful is that it not only provides an environment of curiosity and adventure, but also has the courage to put out products that look and perform quite differently from what we expect.

It all started with the bagless vacuum cleaner in the early 1990s. Based on an idea that Dyson had been working on since the 1970s, the Dual Cyclone went on to become the best-selling vacuum cleaner in Britain, despite being way more expensive than its rivals.

When the Air Multiplier bladeless fan was released in 2009 it was considered 'radical' because it looked so different from what customers expected a fan should. To this day, whenever I see one in a store I can't resist putting my hand through the centre, half amazed not to lose my fingers in the process!

Sir James Dyson, the founder and owner of the company, has been critical of the lack of creativity in the education system: 'Now, we don't teach children in schools to be creative. We don't teach them to experiment. We want them to fill in the right answer, tick the right answer in the box.'

And if we're not teaching children to be creative, why would we expect them to embrace creativity in the workplace?

In her book *The Creativity Formula*, Dr Amantha Imber suggests, 'It is much easier to achieve a creative workforce if the most senior people in the organisation genuinely and actively support and encourage creativity.'

Many cultures are lost in the never-ending cycle of busy work and never make the time to encourage their people to be creative. They don't support them in developing ideas and they lack the courage to bring together directional and intersectional thinkers.

Only when creativity is encouraged do ideas see the light of day, for as Elizabeth Gilbert warns in her book *Big Magic*, 'When courage dies, creativity dies with it.'

CONSTANT CREATIVITY IS THE GOAL

Successful cultural evolution needs a constant stream of ideas to keep it moving forward and to ensure that it doesn't stagnate.

As I've already mentioned, cultural evolution can never be a project, as that implies an end date. There is no end date to culture—it simply is and always will be. Companies that have been around for more than a hundred years, such as Ford, have had to constantly reinvent themselves in order to stay relevant and profitable and to offer their customers something they haven't had before or been able to get from someone else.

Key to this evolution has been finding a way to encourage and collect ideas from its employees.

Toyota's production system, a great example of lean manufacturing, is often used as a case study. Yet what sets Toyota apart is that it spends more time than most of its competitors on building an environment where creativity can flourish and ideas can be captured.

The Toyota Creative Idea Suggestion System, developed by Shoichi Saito in 1951 (after a visit to the Ford plant in Detroit), encouraged all workers to submit their ideas. At that time they were looking for the smallest ideas that could incrementally improve the way the company did things. In post-war Japan the rapidly expanding industry had set course to catch up with and eventually overtake US automotive production. Each idea that was successfully implemented was rewarded; in 1951, 789 suggestions drew rewards totalling $2638.

Yuzo Yasuda has written about the evolution of the system in his book *40 Years, 20 Million Ideas: The Toyota Suggestion System*. I particularly like one anecdote: in 1974, 13 people who received the Gold Prize for Suggestions (given annually) created their own club within the suggestion system. Called the Toyota GI (Good Ideas) Club, it became a place of idea sharing, learning and training, and now has a membership of more than 1000 people.

3M is another organisation that takes creativity seriously and provides its staff with a day a week to think about how to create exciting new products or fix existing problems. This '20% time', as they call it, is seen by most as unrealistic and unachievable, yet with a simple redesignation of low-value work, making time for creative thinking could be within everyone's reach. After all, Apple, Google, Amazon and company wouldn't be where they are now without setting this priority.

CASE STUDY: Uncharted Play

Uncharted Play was founded by Jessica O. Matthews when she was 19 and majoring in psychology and economics at Harvard University. She was driven by a problem that she saw every time she returned home to visit her family in Nigeria.

They had electricity, but because of a lack of funding for infrastructure its supply was hugely unreliable, leaving customers without power for hours on end. So she looked for a simple solution to a big problem.

One thing she noticed was that there was always someone in the street kicking a football, so she started thinking about whether it would be possible to harness the kinetic energy from this play and store it as energy. And just like that the SOCCKET, a soccer ball with a difference, was born, providing a source of cost-efficient renewable energy for the developing world.

Uncharted Play looked to harness kinetic energy from things such as skipping ropes and skateboards. In 2016, Jessica realised that bringing play and power together was good for public relations, but that it wouldn't bring about the changes required to provide real solutions to those living in 'light poverty'. The company was rebranded as Uncharted Power and she raised $7 million in start-up funds.

KEY POINTS

- Being busy is bad for culture, whereas being productive is good.

- Idea generation requires an open mind and rigorous questioning and challenging.

- Create a space where ideas can be shared.

ACTION YOU CAN TAKE

You must allocate time for creativity.

Borrowing from the likes of 3M, Google, Atlassian and others, make creative thinking a priority and provide staff with time to work on any ideas that could fix the smallest of problems. I understand that it isn't possible for every culture to provide its staff with a day a week to do this, but '5% time' is relatively simple to implement; 5 per cent of a 40-hour week is two hours.

I used to do this with my teams. We would set aside 3 pm to 5 pm on a Friday afternoon (when everyone was easing out of 'day-to-day' mode) to challenge a problem we had, perhaps some trivial thing that was holding us back. We used our weekly '5% time' to change things incrementally for the better. We looked at everything we did, wrote our ideas on cards and set about creating more time to implement them.

It was a perfect start for the weekend and ensured our own thinking never became stale.

DATA

The collection of data can greatly enhance the way things get done and the outcomes that are achievable within a culture, provided that the 'right' data is collected and that it's used in the 'right' way.

It seems like only five minutes ago that *big data* projects were all the rage. For those of you with good memories, they came right after Six Sigma but before digital transformation projects in the list of silver bullet solutions to business problems.

Research company Gartner were the first to define what big data meant in a paper in 2001. 'E-commerce, in particular,' they noted, 'has exploded data management challenges along three dimensions: volume, velocity and variety.' They called for IT departments to come up with approaches to dealing with each of these three Vs.

The explosion of social media coupled with the rise in e-commerce transactions led to the generation of more data than the world understood how to process. Hadoop—a network of computers that used massive amounts of data to solve problems—was created in 2005 and allowed organisations to interrogate data in a more structured way and use it to handle a limitless range of tasks.

The expansion of the *internet of things* means more devices are capturing ever more data, leading to usage patterns and greater prediction around customer behaviour. Machine learning is adding further to this.

All of which makes it more important than ever to have strategies for dealing with the three Vs:

- **Volume.** The amount of data captured in a single 'transaction' can lead to terabytes of unstructured information being stored. It's important for an organisation to understand what data they need and how they intend to use it, because storage costs and the potential for data integrity and security issues will increase over time.

- **Velocity.** How quickly does the data need to be captured and used? Technology company Oracle state in their big data guide, 'Normally, the highest velocity of data streams directly into memory versus being written to disk. Some internet-enabled smart products operate in real time or near real time and will require real-time evaluation and action.'

- **Variety.** Getting the most from the data that you capture relies on being able to cope with different types, including text, audio and video. 'Metadata can help to provide contextual consistency to enterprise data,' Gartner suggest, as can 'advanced indexing techniques for relating data of incompatible types'.

Managers around the world want more and more data in order to improve decision making, products and performance, or to find gaps they can exploit, regardless of the organisation or the sector they're in.

Without data it would be hard to know what customers need next, whether new products delivered what was expected, where the weak links are in a system or what part of a culture can be automated.

This last issue is currently the cause of much anxiety, because apparently artificial intelligence (AI) is coming to take everyone's jobs. Machines will be able to process the data more quickly and deliver solutions to problems we don't yet even know we have. They'll be able to work 24/7, won't be distracted by checking their Insta feed and definitely won't ever answer back.

McKinsey estimate that more than US$30 billion is being spent on AI projects, and there's lots of scaremongering around the number of jobs that will be lost to machines. A different report from McKinsey estimates that 400 to 800 million jobs could be lost worldwide by 2030.

So afraid are we of the AI invasion that one question on the subject posted by Balaji Viswanathan on the website Quora.com received more than 300 million views and 4500 answers! He simply asked, 'What would happen if humans lost 50% of all the jobs in the world to robots?'

Are we right to be afraid? Toby Walsh, Professor of AI at Sydney University doesn't think so. At a conference in 2018 he suggested, 'We're a long way from building machines that match the capability of humans. Machines are incredibly slow learners and often need millions of examples to learn from.'

As I mentioned under 'Personality & communication', Walsh's view is that we will eventually teach machines how to do the jobs that we find dirty, dull, difficult and/ or dangerous.

Amazon are trialling drones to deliver parcels, self-driving cars aren't far away from mass production and apps have replaced the decision-making process in many areas, in our house at least!

To do all these things, organisations need data, lots and lots of data. Uber Eats knows I favour vegetarian meals only because I've ordered them so many times. The same is true of Amazon's book recommendations and Netflix's seemingly inexhaustible suggestions of Monty Python shows or similar (nothing is).

'Data is great; data is powerful. I love data,' writes Patty McCord in *Powerful*. 'But the problem is that people become overly wedded to data and too often consider it much too narrowly, removed from the wider business context.'

MAKE DATA ACCESSIBLE BUT SECURE

Something I hear a lot from senior leaders is the need to become 'data driven'. Which is fine, but the reality is that the goal isn't collecting the data, it's using it to make better decisions. So a better way to think of this is in terms of becoming *data informed*.

To become data informed, it has to be provided in a way that makes it accessible to anyone who wants to use it. This is known as data democratisation.

Data federation tools make it possible for it to be aggregated from different places into a virtual database so people can drill down in it further and use it to analyse specific areas of the business.

This is important because otherwise what happens is that different people in different areas capture data and store it in their own personal space (local Excel files being a great example), making it inaccessible to others who might be able to use it.

To make the best use of data, and to use it to grow aspects of the culture, it needs to be shared. In some organisations, certain datasets (such as payroll information) will not be made available, and governance policies will be needed to ensure it cannot be accessed or misused. For everything else — and to demonstrate the trust the organisation has in their employees — data should be made available for business analysis and intelligence.

When this happens people start to get excited about the information at their fingertips and use it creatively to inform innovative projects. Data is critically important to innovation as it provides the fuel that propels ideas forward.

What makes the continuing investment in self-driving cars worthwhile is the data around the number of deaths on the road attributable to driver error. The impetus for Amazon's checkout-free grocery stores is the time it will save customers on their regular shopping trips. (And of course, the money it will make Amazon!)

Making this kind of information available to employees facilitates the ability of cultures to evolve their products, practices and performance. Transformation of anything requires information and turning it into something usable requires people who are great at analytics.

Often these kinds of roles are overlooked or not used in the right way. The technology we have today is fantastic and will only get better, so we need people with analytical skills to ensure that both the data and the tools are easy to use. There's a science to interpreting data, and cultures need to harness it.

All of this is great news, providing you keep it safe. Otherwise you risk undermining not just the culture but the organisation itself. And there are people and organisations desperate to get their hands on as much data as they can get.

In March 2018, the Cambridge Analytica scandal was exposed by the *Observer* newspaper in the UK. In the article whistle-blower Christopher Wylie described how the organisation—at the time owned by the hedge fund billionaire Robert Mercer and run by Steve Bannon, later an adviser to President Trump—harvested the profiles of over 50 million people on Facebook without their permission as part of a campaign to influence American voters in the 2016 presidential election.

The fallout from the scandal eventually led to the liquidation of Cambridge Analytica and forced a not-very-contrite Mark Zuckerberg in front of a not-very-bright congressional hearing. Things got so bad for Facebook that even Elon Musk deleted his account. I know!

The worrying thing about all this is not just the continuing lack of security around the amount of data collected by Facebook, but that it was actually only the seventh largest data security breach reported in 2018!

The number one spot went to the Indian Government whose Aadhaar system, which is used to store biometric information for its citizens, was compromised. For $8, the *Tribune* newspaper was able to gain access to almost one billion (yep, billion) names, addresses, emails and phone numbers in just 10 minutes! All this despite the government declaring two months earlier that 'Aadhaar was fully safe and secure'.

Cyber security has to be a critical part of your strategy, and the culture has to protect the data at all costs. I'm constantly amazed by how many data breaches are caused by careless individuals downloading applications they shouldn't, spreading viruses, or sticking their username and password on a conveniently placed Post-it note!

Cybercriminals will look for any way into the data you hold, and once they're in it's only a matter of time before they find what they're looking for and find a way out again. According to a story in *USA Today*, cyberattacks increased by 32 per cent in 2018 compared with the same period in 2017.

Deloitte, in their paper 'Five Essential Steps to Improve Cyber Security', recommend the following precautions as a minimum for protection against cyber theft:

1. **Focus on what matters.** What critical assets and interactions need to be protected?

2. **Proactively assess your cyber risk.** Become great at knowing what to look for and how to detect emerging threats.

3. **Focus on awareness to build a multilayered defence.** Work collaboratively across the culture to develop defences for everyone who interacts with the data you hold.

4. **Fortify your organisation.** Create an ongoing plan to keep all software and hardware up to date and ensure that physical security is reviewed regularly.

5. **Prepare for the inevitable.** Develop an incident management (and communication) approach in the event of a breach, and test this regularly.

Here are some simple things everyone within the culture can do to play their part:

- Make passwords hard to copy or figure out, and don't write them on a piece of paper and keep them near your computer!

- Don't create generic user accounts and passwords.

- Keep an eye out for anything that looks electronically suspicious. Don't open any email with a dodgy title or from someone you don't know. Oh, and if you do, never open any attachments included.

- Keep all software updated. Scheduling overnight updates is best, so it doesn't impinge on work hours.

- If people are working remotely or from home, ensure they know how to secure data when out of the office.

- Don't take sensitive information out of the office on a portable storage device unless it's encrypted and password protected.

- Close down user accounts when people leave and check users' credentials (what they're allowed access to) regularly.

As with most things in the culture, it's people's behaviour that will ultimately define how safe your information is. However, by making data security a priority within the strategy, investment in time and effort will be established from the outset.

WHAT DOES THE PEOPLE DATA TELL YOU?

One of the most valuable exercises an organisation can undertake to ensure the culture is delivering on the promises made is to run an engagement survey. Surveys provide cultural data that needs to be acted on. It's not enough to collect it and think this proves to staff that the organisation cares. No one buys that.

Just as they see right through the morning teas, celebrations and personal development programs that happen the week before the engagement survey is run. That's like a government promising tax cuts during their election campaign—which is exactly what's happening in Australia as I'm writing this! Talk about timing...

There's a stack of data that can be used to measure how culture is perceived internally, as well as external perceptions of the company and the way it goes about things.

Currently the most popular method for measuring the external customer experience is the Net Promoter Score (NPS), an open-source management tool used by thousands of organisations worldwide (including most of the Fortune 500) to grow their businesses by increasing customer loyalty. At its heart is a metric that measures the willingness of customers to recommend a company's products or services.

An NPS is calculated by asking customers a question along the lines of, 'On a scale of 0 to 10, how likely are you to recommend us to a friend or colleague?' Based on their rating, a customer is categorised as a Detractor (when they give a rating of 6 or below), a Passive (7 or 8) or a Promoter (9 or 10). A score is then calculated by subtracting the percentage of Detractors from the percentage of Promoters.

This results in an NPS ranging from –100 (all your customers think you're rubbish) to +100 (all your customers think you're wonderful).

An NPS survey also always involves one or two follow-up questions asking the customer why they gave the rating they did, and what they would most like to see improved. While the Net Promoter Score enables you to track customer performance over time, the follow-up questions tell you what you need to do to improve it. Beautifully simple. Which is one of the reasons why the NPS has been so successful.

Simplicity should be at the heart of the staff engagement survey too, as asking people within the culture to complete a 300-question survey will guarantee only one thing—apathy.

For an engagement survey to be effective, there needs to be regular constructive feedback, and it needs to be acted on.

Didier Elzinga started life as a computer scientist before spending 13 years in the visual effects industry, the last five years as CEO of Rising Sun Pictures, working on Harry Potter, Superman and Batman movies.

When he thought about where he spent most of his time, though, it was in developing people and culture. So he set about trying to solve the annual performance review problem. He soon realised that most organisations have the tools to understand their customers, but not the staff and the culture.

Back in 2013 customers were paying consultants lots of money to come in and capture what staff thought of the culture, but then the organisations did nothing with it.

From this realisation the people and culture company Culture Amp was born. They received VC funding in 2015 and now have over 2000 customers worldwide, including Pixar, Nike, Cirque de Soleil and the Reserve Bank of San Francisco.

When I spoke with Didier in early 2019, I asked him what a great engagement survey should look like. 'It starts with science,' he said, 'but it's done best by companies that are intentionally describing the experiences they want their people to have, then measuring where its occurring and where it's not.'

The definition part is really important because only then can an organisation find out whether its people are delivering on their promises to each other and, where they're not, what action needs to be taken to resolve the problem. In order to get qualitative feedback, structuring the questions in the right way is critically important, as powerful and honest feedback is needed to move the culture forward.

It's also an assessment of whether or not the people strategy is working. As Didier himself says, 'The culture strategy comes first, then the survey should be part of that.'

What I like most about Culture Amp is that they practise what they preach. They are a company dedicated to using over 20 years' worth of research and thinking to demonstrate to customers that there are multiple answers to the culture question and only through action (not measurement) can meaningful cultural change be achieved.

This is why listening to staff is important, but only by putting money and time behind action can organisations demonstrate the seriousness of their intent to use what they've learned for the good of the culture moving forward.

CASE STUDY: Safaricom

Safaricom is the largest telecommunications company in Kenya and one of the most profitable companies in East and Central Africa, with revenue of over US$2 billion in 2018. It is also ranked as the number one employer in Africa and number 47 in the world in the Forbes Global 200 list of World's Best Employers.

Yet in 2016 it faced a crisis. An unfavourable financial audit was leaked and questions were raised on social media by millennials about the honesty and integrity of CEO Bob Collymore. Rather than get engaged in a war of words, the company decided to listen.

As a result, they launched a new brand, BLAZE, specifically designed for a younger market that includes mentorship programs, youth summits and a TV show dedicated to entrepreneurship. Oh, and you can also customise your phone plan to suit you!

In addition to this, they have staff dedicated to better understanding the spending habits of their customers. They use segmented data to improve the organisation's decision making around the products it offers and to ensure they evolve to meet expected demand.

This data led to the launch of a ride-hailing app to rival Uber, offering lower fares than those of its competitors, a great example of how to use information from customers to diversify and enhance the brand.

KEY POINTS

- Organisations need to think about what data is required and how it will be used.

- All data needs to be secure.

- Collecting people data is good; taking action is better.

ACTION YOU CAN TAKE

Keep the engagement survey simple.

Using tools — like Culture Amp — an organisation can measure whether the culture matches the intent in the people strategy. Whatever you decide to use, keep the questions simple, qualitative and to a minimum. Don't ask people to spend 30–45 minutes answering long-winded questions that require 1000-word answers.

In a vibrant culture, people are likely to take more time to provide more feedback; otherwise, think big, but start small. Qualitative questions should line up to the experiences that employees have or the questions they ask themselves. I always liked closed questions requiring simple yes/no responses as these maximise the number of questions a person can answer in, say, 10–15 minutes.

For example:

- I understand the vision. Y/N

- I see the vision being lived by senior managers. Y/N

- Expectations of me are set clearly. Y/N

- My teammates regularly display the behaviours agreed upon. Y/N

- I recommend the company as a great place to work. Y/N

- I feel safe to contribute my ideas. Y/N

- I have the tools I need to do my job. Y/N

Space should also be provided for people to add more if they feel the need to.

Once completed, the data should be summarised and organised into themes, and the actions built into the following year's people strategy and culture evolution plan. More regular feedback loops provide for faster evolution so are something all cultures should work towards.

FAILURE

It's the sixth of April as I write this and I've just paused for a coffee and a quick scan of the news — and there it is, my current mid-life obsession. While other men my age are out mowing lawns, cleaning their cars, talking about the latest sports results or sleeping off a hangover, I'm in my office reading about Brexit.

No, this isn't going to be a post-mortem on Brexit. It's a discussion about failure, but quite frankly it's hard to separate the two right now.

If you're reading this in 2025 because I haven't bothered to update the book, you might be wondering what all the fuss was about. So let me summarise it for you:

1. UK PM makes concessions to his anti-Europe members by promising a public referendum on whether the country should leave the European Union if the party is re-elected.

2. Party is re-elected.

3. PM follows through on promise of referendum in the hope and expectation that the Leave proposal will be rejected and the Government will be able to quickly move on.

4. Of the 72 per cent of registered voters who participate, 52 per cent vote Leave (after a campaign based on lies

and false numbers, but I digress) and 48 per cent vote Remain.

5. PM resigns.

6. New PM is appointed and—many skirmishes later—presents a 'deal' to Parliament on the conditions under which the UK can leave the European Union.

7. Parliament rejects the deal.

8. PM presents another version of the deal, which is also rejected.

9. Members of Parliament take matters into their own hands and present a range of alternatives to the deal. All are rejected by the House.

10. PM presents a further revision of her deal—and is rejected a third time.

As this manuscript leaves my hands to go into production, I still have no idea how this will all end, but there's no doubt that it's been a litany of failure from start to finish, with no sign of responsible leadership from anyone at any stage. Not from the former Prime Minister, who sold the referendum for votes; or from the current leader, who has stubbornly presented members of Parliament with what amounts to an ultimatum; or from the members themselves, who continue to pursue their own interests rather than those of the people they were elected to represent.

Now, I'm no fan of Brexit (few people are today, according the latest polls), but when did it become okay to deliberately and shamelessly fail the electorate in this way and not accept any kind of responsibility for it?

The willingness to hold one's hand up and admit mistakes is where true leadership is born.

In the Brexit wash-up, thousands of pages will be written describing where things went wrong, but ultimately this failure can only be explained by the behaviours of people and the political culture that exists in the UK today. I want to believe that things will change as a result, that new legislation will be introduced to ensure that some of the things we've seen won't happen again, but I won't be holding my breath, because some cultures seem to thrive on perpetual failure.

Yet failure is not in itself as destructive as this sorry saga suggests. Indeed, failure is something that has to be inherent in cultures, otherwise how will anyone ever know what needs to change, to be improved, to be avoided next time? How will its people learn and develop?

Some of the biggest successes have emerged from failure. The Airbnb story is a good example.

Originally called Air Bed and Breakfast, the idea was for people with spare rooms to throw down air beds and rent them out to people looking for a cheap room.

When first presenting the idea, CEO Brian Chesky received seven funding rejections from prominent Silicon Valley investors. When he made his pitch to an LA designer he held in high regard, the response was, 'Brian, I hope this is not the only thing you're working on'!

As they got further into debt, he and partner Joe Gebbla dreamed up a scheme for creating collectible, themed cereal boxes (nope, I'm not joking) for fictitious breakfast cereals they called 'Obama O's' and 'Cap'n McCains', and the money they raised paid off much of their credit card debt.

They also flew to New York every weekend and went door to door to take hundreds of pictures of apartments to get online.

Today Airbnb operate in more than 34 000 cities and are valued at over US$25 billion. Yet their early failures made them stronger as an organisation and more resilient towards the challenges that they faced as the business evolved.

Different people have different views on failure, though.

Jason Fried, co-founder of web application company Basecamp, comments in Tim Ferriss's book *Tribe of Mentors*, 'Many people will tell you there' a lot to learn from failure, but there's more to learn from success.' Comedian Chris Rock has a different perspective: 'You learn more from fucking up than you do from success. And failure, if you don't let it defeat you, is what fuels your future success.'

And of course they're both right, but in working cultures you have to set the conditions for failure.

MAKE FAILURE OKAY

Don't be fooled by this suggestion. I'm not talking about setting out to deliberately fail—that would be cultural suicide. Scan through some high-profile failures, however, and you start to wonder whether that's what people intended to do.

Facebook phone—remember that? Crystal Pepsi? Those Oakley sunglasses with a built-in MP3 player that cost, like, a million dollars in the early 2000s? Sony minidiscs? That Apple camera that looked like a mini projector/Kodak instamatic hybrid? The Donald Trump–led US Football League?

Of course, these were not deliberate failures, and the people who made them will say (rightly in some instances, though not in the case of the US Football League) that it was something that the company tried and it was valuable research and development that got them closer to doing something different.

But as much as people try to put a positive spin on big product or event fails (hello, Fyre Festival!), if the conditions for failure haven't been set or else the behaviours that lead up to it have been poor, then no matter how many people spin the message that 'failure is good', the impact on people and their morale is going to be bad.

It's a fact that most projects fail (the figure can be as high as 70 per cent) when measured against time and cost expectations. I talked about this extensively in *The Project Book*, and most organisational cultures don't care enough to change it. Instead, they still overpromise or overcommit, and the people at the sharp end are left to carry the emotional and physical strains of delivery.

This kind of failure is not okay. It is a result of poor management, with no leadership in sight. Chasing pipe dreams and taking on too much are indications that those running the company don't have what it takes to make courageous decisions, and in these circumstances the culture fails. It very quickly becomes combatant, then people cease to care and before you know it, it's stagnant and results plummet.

Making failure okay starts with understanding the priorities of the culture and taking the time to list them, thus demonstrating unity and setting the tone for the people doing the work. When people know what's most important, they will make time to do it really well.

An organisation needs to ensure that people know it's okay to take risks and this can be problematic for some, particularly those who like to retain command and control.

A key aspect of becoming more agile or flexible in the way things are done is letting things go and giving a team of motivated people the opportunity to make the decisions they feel are necessary to deliver to the organisation's objectives. In cultures where approval is required from a single person for anything to happen, people won't take risks for fear of making a mistake and having to face the consequences.

These cultures are not psychologically safe and people will always ask for permission, not forgiveness. In high-performing cultures people feel safe to take risks in the knowledge that should they fail, they will learn something new, not be fired or given a public dressing down.

One activity that is becoming more mainstream is the pre-mortem. In a pre-mortem, members of the culture look specifically for ways that something can fail. This exercise is a huge amount of fun (I'll go into it in more detail in the Action section). While the emphasis is on risk management, you also create the conditions for failure to be okay.

Astro Teller (possibly the world's best name, although I recently met someone called Xeno Captain, which is also right up there) is CEO of X, Alphabet's moonshot factory. If you're not familiar with moonshots, they are effectively funded initiatives in science and technology, projects looking to realise ideas that are a little bit magical and out there. So while there are some high-profile successes—driverless cars could be the biggest of them—there are also many abject failures, and at X that's okay.

In a TED talk, Teller spoke of how the teams get excited about failure and actively look for ways to kill something! They have tight feedback loops, so they can learn, and sometimes change direction, quickly.

But shouting at people to fail fast doesn't actually work, he explained. The only way to make it safe is to give the teams the autonomy to run fast at something first, and to ensure that bonuses and rewards are linked to failure as much as to success.

FAILURE IS ABOUT LEARNING

Ultimately the thing that should be celebrated and rewarded is not the failure itself, but the learning it generates. Saying it and doing it are two different things, though, and the message that it's okay to fail needs to be continually reinforced.

The moment blame seeps into the culture is the moment learning ends and failure takes over.

Amy C. Edmondson talked about this in a 2011 *Harvard Business Review* article, 'Strategies for Learning from Failure'. Speaking of leaders, she said, 'They should insist that their organisations develop a clear understanding of what happened—not of "who did it"—when things go wrong.' She suggested five strategies to build a psychologically safe failure culture:

1. **Frame the work accurately.** As I noted under 'Performance management', it's critically important that expectation is set clearly and delivered in a way that the person on the receiving end understands and also feels safe to ask questions to clarify this understanding, if necessary. It's also important that people understand the 'pitfalls', the things that could fail during the course of the action.

2. **Embrace messengers.** Negative doom-mongers are often reviled in cultures as people who are looking for reasons *not* to do something or who *want* something to fail, when more often than not the opposite is true. Being contrarian is valuable and needs to be encouraged and rewarded, as they do at X. Capturing failure then sharing the learning is an important aspect of creating a 'safe to fail' culture.

3. **Acknowledge limits.** When asked what the most important question was when hiring someone for a role, Melanie Silva, Managing Director of Google Australia and New Zealand, chose, ' "Tell me about your biggest failure." The best tell you how they've adapted or changed because of it.' Demonstrating that you're human and fallible and sharing those stories with others creates a rapport that aids collaboration and makes learning easier.

4. **Invite participation.** Another of Amazon's leadership principles is to 'be curious'. 'Leaders are never done learning and always seek to improve themselves. They are curious about new possibilities and act to explore them.' This means continually challenging the way you think about something by bringing in different people with different perspectives to share what they learn.

5. **Set boundaries and hold people accountable.** It's crucial to ensure that everyone within the culture has agreed on the behaviours they'll demonstrate towards each other and the principles they'll apply when working together. When people step outside these boundaries, it is easier to hold each other to account as everyone understands what is and isn't acceptable. When people step outside the organisation's values or continually fail to demonstrate the agreed behaviours and principles, there must be consequences, which are then shared with the team.

A great way to share learning is to create a space where people can post the things they learn through failure. It can be a physical space, like a wall, or a virtual space; it really doesn't matter, as long as people use it and it adds value for those who are about to start something new. It aids the pre-mortem process and creates cultural awareness of the things that have gone before.

Lots of people in the project management world collect 'lessons learned' like my son's bedroom floor collects cast-off clothes. Unfortunately, most of these learnings live in a long and complex spreadsheet that's difficult to navigate and therefore rarely sees the light of day.

My personal preference, which I've witnessed in many great cultures, is a wall in a place that gets a lot of traffic (near the kitchen is always good) with a box of index cards, some blu-tack and felt-tip pens nearby. That way as soon as anyone learns anything, they write it on a card and stick it on the wall. This can become a focal point for a pre-mortem, or a place of quiet learning and reflection.

I'll leave the final word to Laszlo Bock, former SVP of People Operations at Google, who said this in his book *Work Rules: Insights from inside Google that will transform how you live and lead,*

> Celebrating failure is not something that a culture should do. I understand that it's necessary to fail in order to progress, but celebrating the failure isn't the thing to do. Celebrating the learning is. It's a subtle distinction but an important one.

CASE STUDY: Google

No company in the past 20 years has made it more okay to fail than Google. Their list of failures may be longer than their list of successes! If they hadn't created the conditions where it was okay for staff to fail, then they wouldn't have been able to take the risks necessary to grow the business and their culture would have declined as a result. Yet they regularly feature in the employee-voted Glassdoor lists of best places to work.

Their list of failures includes Wave, Inbox, Reader, Talk, Picasa and their attempt at a social network, Google+.

One of the highest profile failures to come out of Alphabet X in the past 10 years was Google Glass. I remember seeing the promo video on YouTube in 2012 and marvelling at the possibilities. I couldn't help but feel there was a sense of 'Opti-Grab' (Google it — they're not doing away with Search any time soon!) about the whole idea, but I got over that.

The concept looked exciting, the way they sold it looked good and the technology seemed to work just fine, but ultimately what seemed to kill Google Glass is that there was really no customer desire for it outside of the fans and early adopters. Sure, there were some great practical things you could do, but let's face it, they looked just a little bit creepy.

Yet the technology has since resurfaced. In mid 2017 *The Guardian* reported that X were working on an industrial reincarnation for Glass and that some organisations (including Boeing) were using the technology in augmented-reality safety goggles.

So while the original project failed, the learnings taken from that have led to more interesting and creative side projects, which may (or may not!) see the light of day after all.

KEY POINTS

- Failure is central to the evolution of cultures.
- Making it okay to fail requires more than words.
- Create spaces and conversations where learnings can be shared.

ACTION YOU CAN TAKE

As I mentioned earlier, one thing every culture can do to get better at becoming more comfortable with failure is to run pre-mortems before starting new work or projects.

This is a technique that is used extensively at Atlassian and as with much of what makes their culture successful, they have shared it in their excellent playbook. Here's an extract that details how they run them, remembering that for it to work well in your culture, you may need to change the terminology or approach to make it successful. The teams at Atlassian use a seven-step process:

1. **Set the stage.** Make sure people are clear on the scope of the work because that's the scope of your discussion for the next 90 minutes. Now choose an actual date in the future. It could be a few days, weeks or months past your launch date, depending on the size and length of the work.

2. **Glass half full/empty.** A failure team brainstorms all the reasons that the work could fail ('prospective hindsights'). A success team does likewise, brainstorming all the ways it could succeed or exceed expectations. Similar themes are then sought in each team.

3. **Cross-examine.** A member of each team is asked to summarise the ideas or themes they found. The other team gets to ask thought-provoking questions in order to push one another to come up with more risks or opportunities.

4. **Vote.** Everyone then votes on the top three risks or opportunities for the work. Everyone gets three votes and is asked to focus on outcomes that can be influenced.

5. **Make a plan.** Back in the groups, the failure team looks at how they will tackle the top three rated risks and the success team handles the opportunities. The emphasis is on practical action, not ambiguous goals.

6. Assign owners. Responsibilities are assigned to ensure that plans are followed through.

7. Capture and share. The outcomes are captured and a place created where they can be shared.

MAKING CULTURE STICK

Organisations talk a lot about change and transformation, but in general they aren't very good at putting it into practice. A recent SAP survey found that of the 84 per cent of organisations that started transformation initiatives in the past year, only 3 per cent had actually successfully completed one.

One reason for this is that while senior managers get very excited about smarter, faster ways of doing things when they're pulling their business plans together, they forget that to achieve them they have to stop doing some things and redefine the way they get others done.

Cultural evolution is frequently cited as the biggest enabler of successful change, yet very few organisations ever take it on, opting instead (as I've described) for quick-fix training solutions, restructures or funky office fit-outs.

Yet every project undertaken, regardless of the method used to deliver it, provides an opportunity to move from one cultural state to another. From opening a new office to implementing a new policy to increasing grade averages — whatever it is — there'll be something new or different at the end and people have to be ready for it.

To successfully prepare people for cultural evolution a few things need to be in place.

- **A sound business case for change.** This will answer the 'why this and why now?' questions and provide a foundation on which the activity required to deliver the change can be built. It's not enough simply to say 'we need to change our culture'; as for any other change, there needs to be a sound rationale that people buy into.

- **Public accountability.** There needs to be a senior executive within the business who is prepared to throw their reputation and effort behind the activity and ensure it delivers what was promised in the case for change. This person will encourage all the other executives do their bit to ensure that the change happens.

- **A strong team.** Built at the start of the project, the team will work collaboratively to deliver value (as outlined in the case for change) as quickly as is possible to satisfy the needs of the organisation. The team will be diverse and inclusive and may sometimes require external expertise to facilitate a process, then short bursts of inspiration, motivation and new thinking.

- **A strong vision and definition of the future state.** As outlined early in the book, to motivate and inspire a team and ensure that those using the outputs from the initiative understand what's required of them, a vision, a set of values and a description of the future are required, so people understand what they're asked to be a part of.

- **Clear, unambiguous communication.** This should focus on the activities required to complete the initiative, but also on the personal change required to achieve success. I don't mean an email or poster, in Comic Sans font, pinned up on a noticeboard, but regular effort from those accountable for the cultural evolution.

When it comes to communication, if the people within the culture don't believe in the change, aren't involved in it, don't feel part of it or simply don't understand it, it will fail. Similarly, if people get in the way of change and there's no consequence for doing so, it will fail.

Here's where great change managers can add the most value:

- They understand that cultural evolution requires a different level of energy and actively lead the team-building work at the beginning of the initiative to ensure it starts with the right intention.

- They work closely with those accountable and responsible for delivery and ensure that messages are delivered in a way that stakeholders understand.

- They help people move away from the familiar to the often uncomfortable 'new' way of doing things.

- They coach, mentor and remind people of the cultural evolution that's required. They hold them to the required behaviours and ensure the right path is followed by those who may be standing in the way.

- They are realistic optimists and help people to see the medium- to long-term positives of the change. They are empathetic, honest, trustworthy, disciplined and resilient, and they build influence across the organisation.

Cultural evolution occurs every day, whether there is activity or not, and organisations can utilise their change managers to help them do this positively. They may not be formal roles, but instead a network of people who act as catalysts for change.

One of the tools they can use to do this that captures the intent of the refreshed culture is the *culture deck*.

ALL HANDS ON DECK

The culture deck trend was made famous by Netflix in 2009. It serves as a social contract for staff, describing the future state and explaining the responsibilities of the organisation and the individual in the business of achieving it. Patty McCord, who co-created the culture deck with CEO Reed Hastings, said in a podcast, 'I don't know if [the Netflix culture] was so different. Here's the most important thing we did: We just wrote it down.'

Social contracts are not new. One of the earliest expositions of social contract theory was offered by the English philosopher Thomas Hobbes in the mid 17th century. At that time England was torn apart by a civil war that pitted against each other two fundamentally opposed ideas of government: one by absolute royal fiat and divine right, the other in which popular representation through Parliament played a role.

It was in this context that Hobbes wrote *Leviathan*, in which he explored what it means to establish a civilised society in the absence of political order. Essentially, he believed that 'order', in and of itself, exists only when people who are part of a culture define what it is. 'Political authority and obligation,' he argued,

> are based on the individual self-interests of members of society who are understood to be equal to one another, with no single individual invested with any essential authority to rule over the rest. Government is only legitimate when its citizens have consented to it.

Social contract theory would be explored further by philosophers such as Samuel von Pufendorf (1673), Jean-Jacques Rousseau (1762) and Immanuel Kant (1797), the latter immortalised in Monty Python's 'The Philosopher's Song' ... but I digress.

John Locke (1689) had rather different ideas on social contract theory, but agreed on the central point that those in a 'state of nature' (whose actions are not bound by arbitrary government or laws but by reason alone) must negotiate a mutually agreed social contract. Locke's belief that 'rational' people favour organised government, under which every citizen should be treated equally, deeply influenced the authors of the United States Declaration of Independence.

So what has all this historical stuff got to do with culture? Well, the culture deck is the document that describes the state of nature for the organisation and thus the social rules all members agree to respect.

The culture deck generally describes:

- vision
- values
- behaviours
- principles of collaboration
- measures of success
- why people would want to work there
- development opportunities for staff.

This document is produced at the end of the culture definition process and is a result of the efforts of a cross-section of all staff whom it represents.

When I run the culture definition activity for smaller cultures, this could entail all (let's say) 20 members of staff; for larger cultures, 200 staff may represent 2000 employees. Senior executives are part of this group, but do not have a dominant voice. Each of them, after all, is just one representative of the culture with the same voting rights as everyone else.

When done well the culture deck can provide:

- improved communication
- more empathy
- improved collaboration
- greater acceptance of accountability and responsibility

- greater challenge
- increased diversity
- improved creativity.

Culture decks come in all shapes and sizes, and are always co-created by all members of the culture. Key to their success, though, is their simplicity, in both presentation and language.

Netflix's original culture deck ran to 125 pages, which is a pretty long read in my opinion. Nordstrom, by contrast, state, 'Our employee handbook is a single card that says "Use good judgement in all situations".' Zappos' first culture book consisted of 100 words from each employee on the company culture.

Different organisations call their culture decks different things. PossibleHealth call theirs a culture code, Disqs a culture book, Hootsuite a manifesto, IDEO 'The Little Book of IDEO'.

They all do the same thing, though: they describe the culture in enough detail that every employee (incumbent or prospective) understands what it takes to contribute to the success of the organisation. Bretton Putter, author of *Culture Decks Decoded*, also said in an article for *Entrepreneur* magazine, 'Culture decks serve as the ideological anchor of the company that allow people to call BS on leaders' actions.'

Drawing up the culture deck is one thing; having the discipline to stick to it is quite another, and this is where teams will rely on their collective emotional intelligence to hold themselves to their own rules.

MAKE CULTURAL EVOLUTION BUSINESS AS USUAL

Creating a culture deck is the first—not the last—part of cultural evolution. It doesn't end when the deck is in place;

that's when it starts. Once it's published, it's there to be built on. 'Creating a culture is an evolutionary process,' says Patty McCord. 'Think of it as an experimental journey of discovery.'

Because of the ever-changing nature of culture, new ideas, thinking and people need to be regularly injected into it to ensure that everyone has the necessary skills and that it maintains relevance and continues to meet the changing requirements of the organisation.

A regular program of activity should be built, ensuring that the values are lived and the behaviours upheld. These sessions could be as simple as 'Essential Meeting Skills' or 'Facilitation Skills'. Other essential skills that people will need to be equipped with include:

- providing feedback
- communicating to different personalities
- keeping things simple
- being the most emotionally intelligent version of oneself
- managing risk
- running a hackathon
- being resilient
- keeping stakeholders satisfied
- active listening.

HR departments often provide these kinds of learning and development programs. In my experience, however, bringing together larger groups for micro-learning sessions so they can discuss *how* to do these things within the context of the culture work they need to do, and to agree how they'll hold each other to account, is much more effective.

A series of brown bag lunches where others within the culture share their experiences, the things that have worked well and the things that haven't, is another great way to make cultures vibrant. It's also an opportunity to celebrate success and eat food—two of my favourite activities.

Vibrant cultures never stand still, and a new role is emerging to ensure that doesn't happen.

Marketing organisation Mailchimp are just one example of an organisation that has established a 'Chief Culture Officer', who has the responsibility to ensure that the culture is defined, that people are hired for values fit and that new skills continue to be introduced.

This person is the custodian of the culture and makes sure that it never becomes stagnant. And before you think, 'That's awesome, we should do that immediately!', just remember that the title isn't important, it's what gets done that counts. Navigating change isn't easy. It requires empathy, flexibility, resilience, great communication and no end of energy, because moving to a cycle of continual evolution will be hard for most people.

In his book *Managing Transitions* (published in 1992), William Bridges created a model that identified three stages of change and detailed the impact of each stage on people. This model remains relevant to almost every culture evolution activity today.

The three transition stages are as follows:

- **Stage 1: Ending, losing and letting go.** Asking someone to give up what they are familiar with and move to something new can be incredibly difficult to do, even if you've gone about it in the right way. They may feel anger, denial, uncertainty and frustration; they may also be scared about what the future holds. Empathy is required at this stage—there'll need to be lots of listening.

  It's completely unreasonable to expect someone to understand and accept change overnight. They need to be involved in the new activity, their concerns need to be heard and understood, and they need time to process it.

'Mandating' any change unlocks the inner child in people. They will resist it and their resistance should be respected. In order for them to move on to the next stage they need to be able to accept that change is happening and then make the choice to be part of it or not.

- **Stage 2: The neutral zone.** There is often lots of confusion, impatience and uncertainty in this zone. People have let go of some of the things they considered normal and have accepted that change is imminent. Some people will want it done quickly; others may still want to be convinced, and this can lead to widespread frustration.

  Constant reinforcement of the value of the change and the future goals is critical here so employees understand the culture's medium- and longer-term goals. Any attempts made by people to 'go back' need to be managed, and those responsible for motivating others on the change initiatives will need high levels of resilience and may start to sound like a broken record.

- **Stage 3: The new beginning.** By this stage, energy and excitement should be high. There should be commitment to the changes afoot and a number of initiatives will have been completed. People will be asking questions, be enthusiastic about new approaches and look for opportunities to learn more.

  They'll willingly give up their time for others, and collaboration will happen across the culture. Engagement scores will lift, as will performance and results, and the payback on the cultural evolution activity will be tangible.

Bridges' Transition Model is just one of many out there that speak to the impact of cultural change on people. You should never lose sight of the fact that that's why many organisations avoid cultural evolution. So in the end they rebrand or send everyone on a training course and hope for the best.

Who better to lead a cultural evolution program than Personnel, Human Resources, People and Culture, the Staff Experience team—or whatever they happen to be called by the time you read this.

Some of my own personal experiences include their dissuading me from performance managing staff (which happened in more than one organisation) because it would be 'hard to do'; taking forever to process paperwork to get new people through the door, then not providing a streamlined welcoming schedule when those people start their jobs; never challenging the internal procedures around performance reviews; and allowing personal development budgets to be cut, rather than standing up for the people they're supposed to represent.

Writing this now it feels unfair, as I've had a fair few run-ins with other departments too and they weren't all bad. Mostly they were underwhelming, yet at the same time I had a degree of empathy for them. For a long time now they've been the only voice at the top table arguing for leadership and culture programs, only to see them ignored in favour of other executives' pet projects or an underinvestment in people and their environment.

More and more organisations are recognising that the evolution of culture is simply the most important thing that a business can invest in.

I believe it's desperately important for HR to be more forceful around the need for culture investment and to become the role models that managers need them to be. With this in mind I sought out the opinion of someone who lives in this world and understands the challenges better than I do. I asked CIPD Membership Director David D'Souza about the role of the HR department moving forward.

'This is a really good time for HR,' David said.

> The dominant narratives around culture, mental health and wellbeing, diversity and inclusion — HR can help and make a difference. But they can't afford to be passive. They need to step forward to the challenges they face.

Evolving culture needs to reflect the collective will of the senior leadership team. It's easy for others to say about culture, 'That's HR's problem to deal with', yet everyone has a responsibility. As David said, 'HR can't be the moral compass of an organisation. If it is, the organisation has lost already, as one voice can't sway them.'

He's right.

Cultural evolution means full-on systemic change of almost everything within an organisation. It's about priorities, communication, decisions, success, failure and the stories the people tell each other about it.

Culture, when done well, is a thing to behold, celebrate and share. The question is whether you have the guts to take it on. Those who do will reap the rewards outlined in 'The value of culture'. Head back there then ask yourself, 'How much do I want it?'

CASE STUDY: Shop Direct Group

The last organisation I worked for in the UK was Shop Direct Group. Formed from a merger between retail companies Littlewoods and Kays Group, they'd seen their catalogue-based sales decline as a result of a rise in online shopping. ASOS.com in particular had risen to prominence, and the Barclay Brothers–owned business was on the verge of irrelevance.

In 2005 they undertook a program to fully modernise the business and change its culture to one that was focused on embracing digital transactions and automation, and to move away from its core business and put everything online.

This involved new and upgraded distribution centres, new contracts with overseas suppliers, updated processes and roles, new office spaces and upgraded technology, and it all had to be done within three years.

The then Managing Director Mark Newton-Jones put the emphasis on rebuilding the culture first, while also building relationships with key suppliers to help transform the business. As a member of the extended leadership team, I was one of more than 300 people who attended a two-day off-site working collaboratively with other members of the organisation to redefine the vision statement and to determine the behaviours we needed to demonstrate to make the transformation program a success.

The vision was used to guide everything we did, the behaviours were embraced in every department, and the goal to become the UK's largest online retailer was achieved. There were tough decisions along the way, with redundancies and traditional services lost, yet throughout it all there was a sense of affinity and collaboration that has stayed with me to this day.

KEY POINTS

- Change managers aid the process of cultural evolution.

- A culture deck can help to capture the aspirations and define the detail of the culture.

- Cultural evolution should be business as usual and the responsibility of everyone on the senior management team, not just HR.

ACTION YOU CAN TAKE

Once the new culture has been defined it's important to maintain the momentum, as simply talking about it won't be enough to keep energy and commitment levels high.

A structured program of events should be created to introduce a different kind of energy and new thinking, and to provide an opportunity for action. This could include celebrating success, providing praise, mixing socially, introducing a coach or simply inviting in an external speaker over lunch.

Having a program like this will help people to see and understand the new beginning. It will help heal the hurt, and reduce confusion and uncertainty, by demonstrating the organisational commitment to the new approach.

Taking the time and effort to define the culture is a great first step; supporting people to change their mindset and skills to make it stick is the crucial second step.

REFERENCES

Preface

John R. Graham et al., 'Corporate culture: Evidence from the field', *NBER Working Paper no. 23255*, issued March 2017.

What is culture?

Global Human Capital Trends 2016, 'The new organization: Different by design', Deloitte University Press.

IDC Forecasts Worldwide Spending on Digital Transformation Technologies to Reach $1.3 Trillion in 2018, IDC, Framingham, Mass., 15 December 2017.

McKinsey & Company, 'Culture for a digital age', *McKinsey Quarterly*, July 2017.

Atlassian Teamwork, 'Welcome your newest teammate … AI. Why healthy teamwork will make or break your success in adapting to this new world', n.d.

Victor Lipman, 'Study explores drivers of employee engagement', *Forbes*, 14 Dec 2012.

Robert Safian, 'Exclusive: Spotify CEO Daniel Ek on Apple, Facebook, Netflix — and the future', *Fast Company*, 7 August 2018.

Stanislav Maleshkov, 'The 5 main domains of emotional intelligence', LinkedIn, 7 October 2014.

The value of culture

ING, 'ING posts 2017 net result of EUR 4,905 million; 4Q17 net result of EUR 1,015 million', Amsterdam, 31 January 2018.

Gallup, *State of the American Workplace Report 2017.*

PwC, '20 years inside the mind of the CEO ... What's next?', *20th CEO Survey*, 2017.

Tatyana Shumsky, 'U.S. consulting fees climb to $63.2 billion in 2017 on tax, digital transformation', *Wall Street Journal*, 6 June 2018.

Derek Sivers, 'How to start a movement', TED 2010.

Antonio Losada and Javier Bajer, 'How we transformed our culture in 100 days: The story behind an intensive culture change program at HSBC Argentina', *Strategic HR Review*, *8*(5), 18–22, 2009.

Cultures & subcultures

PwC, 'Capital project and infrastructure spending: Outlook to 2025', Oxford Economics, 2014.

PMI, 'Success in disruptive times: expanding the value delivery landscape to address the high cost of low performance', *Pulse of the Profession 2018.*

'The Spotify playbook', The Agile Warrior blog, 21 November 2017.

Personality & communication

Justin Kruger and David Dunning, 'Unskilled and unaware of it: How difficulties in recognizing one's own incompetence lead to inflated self-assessments', *Journal of Personality and Social Psychology*, 77(6), 1121–34, January 2000.

David Zes, 'A better return on self-awareness', *Briefings Magazine,* Korn Ferry Institute, 18 November 2013.

Megan Beck and Barry Libert, 'The rise of AI makes emotional intelligence more important', *Harvard Business Review,* 15 February 2017.

Lauren Weber and Elizabeth Dwoskin, 'Are workplace personality tests fair?', *Wall Street Journal,* 29 September 2014.

Laura Janusik, 'Listening facts', International Listening Association, n.d.

Jason Marsh, 'Do mirror neurons give us empathy?', *Greater Good Magazine,* 29 March 2012.

The Cultural Web, 'Aligning your organization's culture with strategy', n.d.

Culture Amp, '6 ways to foster belonging in the workplace: Taking Diversity & Inclusion to the next level', 2017.

Great Place to Work, 'World's best workplaces 2018, 20. Admiral Group', 15 October 2018.

Vision

Robert Safian, 'Exclusive: Spotify CEO Daniel Ek on Apple, Facebook, Netflix — and the future', *Fast Company,* 7 August 2018.

The Cultural Web, 'Aligning your organization's culture with strategy', n.d.

Alannah Eileen Rafferty and Mark Griffin, 'Dimensions of transformational leadership: Conceptual and empirical extensions', *The Leadership Quarterly, 15*(3), 329–54, June 2004.

Laurent-Pierrre Baculard et al., 'Orchestrating a successful digital transformation', Bain and Company, 22 November 2017.

Joe McKendrick, 'Digital transformation, defined by the AWS transformers', *ZDNet*, 1 August 2018.

Lovell Corporation, 'How Millennials and Generation Z are redefining work', *The Change Generation® Report*, 2017.

4 A's, '5 Questions for: Luis Montero, President of the community', 25 September 2016.

'Best places to work 2019', *Advertising Age*, 7 January 2019.

'*Advertising Age*'s prestigious A-List: Progressive cross-cultural agency translates name to the community', *BusinessWire*, 26 January 2016.

Values

Denise Lee Yohn, 'Ban these 5 words from your corporate values statement', *Harvard Business Review*, 5 February 2018.

Volkswagen Annual Report 2015.

Graeme Wearden and Julia Kollewe, 'VW emissions scandal: Misconduct, process failure and tolerance of rule-breaking blamed — as it happened', *The Guardian* (Aus.), 11 December 2015.

Zappos Insights 2018, 'Zappos onboarding fact sheet'.

Victoria Fitoussi, 'Top 10 employee onboarding programs', *Sapling*, 1 March 2019.

'Elite SEM ranked #1 Best Place to Work by *Ad Age*', Cision PR Newswire, 7 January 2019.

'How Ben Kirshner brought meritocracy to digital marketing', Mixergy interview transcript, 13 July 2016.

Behaviour

Laura Reave, 'Spiritual values and practices related to leadership effectiveness', *The Leadership Quarterly*, *16*(5), 655–87, October 2005.

Laurent-Pierrre Baculard et al., 'Orchestrating a successful digital transformation', Bain and Company, 22 November 2017.

Jacques Bughin et al., 'The case for digital reinvention', *McKinsey Quarterly*, February 2017.

Julie Goran et al., 'Culture for a digital age', *McKinsey Quarterly*, July 2017.

Jon Katzenbach and Ashley Harshak, 'Stop blaming your culture', *strategy+business*, 19 January 2011.

'Google paid off top male execs facing sexual harassment claims, lawsuit says', stuff.co.nz, 13 March 2019.

Andrew Sparrow, 'Sept 11: "A good day to bury bad news"', *The Telegraph*, 10 October 2001.

George Jones, 'Police question Blair on honours', *The Telegraph*, 15 December 2006.

J. Miranda and R. V. Brody, 'Communicating bad news', *Western Journal of Medicine*, *156*(1), 83–5, January 1992.

McKinsey & Company, 'ING's agile transformation', *McKinsey Quarterly*, January 2017.

Recognition & reward

Andrew Das, 'U.S. women's soccer team sues U.S. Soccer for gender discrimination', *New York Times*, 8 March 2019.

John Parkinson, 'Dems renew push for equal pay for equal work: "Time that we pay people what they are worth" ', *ABC News*, 30 January 2019.

Fortune editors, 'These are 2018's world's best workplaces', *Fortune*, 15 October 2018.

Performance management

Allison Scott et al., 'Tech leavers study: A first-of-its-kind analysis of why people voluntarily left jobs in tech', Kapor Center for Social Impact, 27 April 2017.

Alison Mau, 'Majority of women MPs suffer "violence and harassment" in Parliament: report', stuff.co.nz, 31 January 2019.

Jamie Ensor, 'Prime Minister Jacinda Ardern says she's been sexually harassed on multiple occasions', *Newshub*, 23 January 2019.

Liz Ryan, 'Performance reviews are pointless and insulting — so why do they still exist?', *Forbes*, 24 January 2019.

Marcus Buckingham and Ashley Goodall, 'Reinventing performance management, *Harvard Business Review*, April 2015.

Salvador Rodriguez, 'Inside Facebook's "cult-like" workplace, where dissent is discouraged and employees pretend to be happy all the time', CNBC, 8 January 2019.

Boris Ewenstein et al., 'Ahead of the curve: The future of performance management', *McKinsey Quarterly*, May 2016.

Center for Creative Leadership, 'Lead-it-yourself solutions, workshop kits, feedback that works', n.d.

Robert Safian, 'Exclusive: Spotify CEO Daniel Ek on Apple, Facebook, Netflix — and the future', *FastCompany*, 7 August 2018.

Diversity & inclusion

Atlassian, 2018 State of Diversity and Inclusion in U.S. Tech, Stats Summary.

Clear Company, '10 diversity statistics that will make you rethink your hiring decisions', April 2019.

Alex Dibble, 'Proportion of British BAME players has doubled since the Premier League began' — talkSPORT special report, 15 August 2017.

Allison Scott et al., 'Tech leavers study: A first-of-its-kind analysis of why people voluntarily left jobs in tech', Kapor Center for Social Impact, 27 April 2017.

Michelle V. Rafter, 'Textio CEO Kieran Snyder on the importance of language', Talent Economy, 2018.

Alison Reynolds and David Lewis, 'Teams solve problems faster when they're more "cognitively diverse"', *Harvard Business Review*, 30 March 2017.

Netflix Jobs, Inclusion & Diversity.

Q & A with Scott E. Page, Princeton University Press.

Janine Schindler and Forbes Coaches Council, 'The benefits of cognitive diversity', *Forbes*, 26 November 2018.

Culture Amp, '6 ways to foster belonging in the workplace: Taking Diversity & Inclusion to the next level', 2017.

Great Place to Work, 'World's Best Workplaces 2018, 4. Intuit', 15 October 2018.

Ben Smith, 'What we're doing to keep building a diverse editorial operation', BuzzFeed, 2 October 2014.

Collaboration

Deloitte Insights, 'The rise of the social enterprise', *2018 Deloitte Global Human Capital Trends*, Deloitte University Press.

Julia Rozovsky, 'The five keys to a successful Google team', *re:Work*, 17 November 2015.

Relly Nadler, '10 reasons why teams need emotional intelligence', *Psychology Today*, 6 July 2017.

Deloitte, 'Rewriting the rules for the digital age', *2017 Deloitte Global Human Capital Trends*, Deloitte University Press.

Matthew Lieberman and Naomi Eisenberger, 'The pains and pleasures of social life: A social cognitive neuroscience approach', *NeuroLeadership*, n.d.

Fiona Robertson, 'What if Maslow was wrong? AKA: Why are cultures so sticky?', LBD Group, 14 January 2019.

Lee Turner and Gary Kenward, 'Preparing to receive patients with trauma', *Nursing Times*, 10 September 2002.

Process & compliance

McKinsey & Company, 'How to create an agile organization', October 2017 Survey.

Ron Jeffries, 'Developers should abandon agile', blog, 10 May 2018.

Jason Bloomberg, 'How DBS Bank became the best digital bank in the world by becoming invisible', *Forbes*, 23 December 2016.

Systems & tools

Shmula, Jeff Bezos interview on defect reduction and Lean and Six Sigma, shmula.com, 7 October 2007.

Mengqi Sun, 'Businesses predict digital transformation to be biggest risk factor in 2019', *Wall Street Journal*, 5 December 2018.

Singapore Management University, *Cultural transformation in the digital world*, research report, November 2018.

Atlassian, 'You waste a lot of time at work'.

Radicati Group, Email Statistics Report, 2019–2023.

Nenad Maljković, 'The email charter: An idea worth spreading', *Medium*, 9 February 2018.

Tom Gimbel, 'My entire company avoids email for one full day every quarter', *FastCompany*, 5 July 2017.

Working environment

Jena McGregor, 'Open office plans are as bad as you thought', *Washington Post*, 18 July 2018.

Sue Shellenbarger, 'Don't get too used to your own desk', *Wall Street Journal*, 15 May 2018.

The Saylor Foundation, 'Scientific management theory and the Ford Motor Company'.

Geoffrey James, 'It's official: Open-plan offices are now the dumbest management fad of all time, *Inc.*, 16 July 2018.

Jenna Goudreau, 'Back to the Stone Age? New Yahoo CEO Marissa Mayer bans working from home', *Forbes*, 25 February 2013.

Corporate Rebels, 'The most pioneering workplace in the Middle East', 12 January 2019.

Innovation

Amantha Imber, '5 ways to create a culture of innovation', Atchub.net, 31 May 2016.

Scott Kirsner, 'The biggest obstacles to innovation in large companies', *Harvard Business Review*, 30 July 2018.

Ellen Huet and Olivia Zaleski, 'Silicon Valley's $400 juicer may be feeling the squeeze', Bloomberg, 19 April 2017.

Ben Tarnoff, 'America has become so anti-innovation — it's economic suicide', *The Guardian*, 11 May 2017.

Deloitte, 'Rewriting the rules for the digital age', *2017 Deloitte Global Human Capital Trends*, Deloitte University Press.

Julie Goran et al., 'Culture for a digital age', *McKinsey Quarterly*, July 2017.

Jeffrey H. Dyer et al., 'The innovator's DNA', *Harvard Business Review*, December 2009.

Soumitra Dutta et al., 'Energizing the world with innovation', *Global Innovation Index 2018*, 11th edn.

Sean Tang and David Aycan, 'How to set the conditions for innovation', *IDEO*, 6 July 2018.

Creativity

APS, Illuminations: Special Edition on Innovation in Organisations, November 2012, Australian Psychological Society.

Dominick Quartuccio, 'We live in the golden era of Lazy Busy', Thrive Global, 17 March 2018.

Data

Doug Laney, '3D data management: Controlling data volume, velocity, and variety', Application Delivery Strategy Meta Group, 6 February 2001.

Oracle, 'What is Big Data?', oracle.com.

McKinsey Global Institute, 'Artificial Intelligence — the next digital frontier?', discussion paper, McKinsey & Company, June 2017.

James Manyika et al., 'Jobs lost, jobs gained: What the future of work will mean for jobs, skills, and wages', November 2017 report, McKinsey & Company.

Jon Walker, 'The self-driving car timeline – predictions from the top 11 global automakers', Emerj, 14 May 2019.

Carole Cadwalladr and Emma Graham-Harrison, 'Revealed: 50 million Facebook profiles harvested for Cambridge Analytica in major data breach', *The Guardian*, 18 March 2018.

Martin Hron, 'Top 10 biggest data breaches in 2018', Avast blog, 20 December 2018.

Rachna Khaira, 'Rs 500, 10 minutes, and you have access to billion Aadhaar details', *The Tribune* (India), 5 January 2018.

Mike Snider, 'Your data was probably stolen in cyberattack in 2018 — and you should care', *USA Today*, 28 December 2018.

Deloitte, 'Five essential steps to improve cyber security', deloitte.com/za.

Abdi Latif Dahir, 'The CEO of Africa's most innovative mobile company warns his "clumsy" product needs to diversify or risk dying', *Quartz Africa*, 21 October 2015.

Lily Kuo, 'To reach millennial customers, this Kenyan telecom giant tried shopping like them', *Quartz Africa*, 12 September 2016.

Duncan Miriri and Neha Wadekar, 'Kenya's Safaricom launches Little Cab app to rival Uber', Reuters, 5 July 2016.

Nik Gowing and Chris Langdon, 'How to thrive on change', *Entrepreneur Asia Pacific*, 6 December 2018.

Failure

Derek Thompson, 'Airbnb CEO Brian Chesky on building a company and starting a "sharing" revolution', *The Atlantic*, 13 August 2013.

CB Insights Research Briefs, 'When corporate innovation goes bad — the 141 biggest product failures of all time', 19 December 2018.

Astro Teller, 'The unexpected benefits of celebrating failure', TED 2016.

Amy C. Edmondson, 'Strategies for learning from failure', *Harvard Business Review*, April 2011.

Melanie Silver interview, 'Why Google chief Melanie Silva wants to hear your failures', *Australian Financial Review*, 7 March 2019.

John Naughton, 'The rebirth of Google Glass shows the merit of failure', *The Guardian*, 23 July 2017.

Making culture stick

Adi Gaskell, 'The slow pace of digital transformation', *Forbes*, 8 June 2018.

Knowledge@Wharton, 'Learning from Netflix: How to build a culture of freedom and responsibility', Interview with Patty McCord, 29 May 2018.

Blake Morgan, 'Chief culture officer and chief customer officer: A winning combination', *Forbes*, 16 January 2018.

ACKNOWLEDGEMENTS

Huge thanks to the following people. Some provided data for me to use. Some gave up their time to talk to me. Some share their research and ideas. Some make me laugh out loud and listen to my boring stories. Some inspire me from a distance. The contents of this book would have been poorer without your direct and indirect input.

Jodie Reynoldson

Dom Price

David D'Souza

Didier Elzinga

Gary Vaynerchuk

Tim Ferriss

Seth Godin

Richard Branson

Josh Bersin and the team at Bersin by Deloitte

The team that produce the Atlassian blog

The team that produce the Culture Amp blog

The team that produce the IDEO blog

Lisa O'Neill

And everyone who takes the time to share things that continue to inspire me to write and deliver.

Thank you all.

SOUNDTRACK

Arctic Monkeys, *Tranquillity Base Hotel & Casino*

Broods, *Don't Feed the Pop Monster*

Depeche Mode, *Songs of Faith and Devotion*

DMA's, *For Now*

Elbow, *The Seldom Seen Kid*

Frazier Chorus, *Sue*

Gruff Rhys, *Babelsberg*

I Know Leopard, *Love Is a Landmine*

Imogen Heap, *The Music of Harry Potter and the Cursed Child*

Japanese Wallpaper, *Japanese Wallpaper*

Jean Michel Jarre, *Equinoxe*

Logic, *Supermarket*

London Grammar, all albums

Methyl Ethyl, *Triage*

Parcels, *Parcels*

Public Service Broadcasting, *The Pit*

Public Service Broadcasting, *The Race for Space*

Public Service Broadcasting, *White Star Liner*

Queen, *Greatest Hits*

R.E.M., *In Time: The Best of R.E.M.*

R.E.M., *Up*

Radiohead, *A Moon Shaped Pool*

Rolling Coastal Blackouts Fever, *Hope Downs*

Scott Walker, *Scott, Scott 2, 3* and *4*

Suede, *Suede*

The Beatles, *Revolver*

The Cure, *Staring at the Sea: The Singles*

The Happy Mondays, *Pills, Thrills and Bellyaches*

The Lu Lu Raes, *Lulu*

The O'Jays, *Backstabbers*

The Smiths, all albums (yep, all of them)

The Stone Roses, *Made of Stone*

The Stone Roses, *The Stone Roses*

The Tea Street Band, *Frequency*

Whitney Houston, *The Ultimate Collection*

BOOKLIST

Adam Alter, *Irresistible: The Rise of Addictive Technology and the Business of Keeping Us Hooked*

Laszlo Bock, *Work Rules! Insights from Google That Will Transform How You Live and Lead*

Brené Brown, *Rising Strong*

James P. Carse, *Finite and Infinite Games*

Daniel Coyle, *The Culture Code*

Mihaly Csikszentmihalyi, *Flow*

Dr Carol Dweck, *Mindset*

Tim Ferriss, *Tribe of Mentors*

Victor Frankl, *Man's Search for Meaning*

Jason Fried & David Hannemeir Hanson, *ReWork*

Gerd Gigerenzer, *Gut Feelings: The Intelligence of the Unconscious*

Seth Godin, *Tribes*

Daniel Goleman, *Emotional Intelligence*

Thich Nhat Hanh, *The Art of Living*

Yuval Noah Harari, *Homo Deus*

Yuval Noah Harari, *Sapiens*

Patrick Hollingworth, *The Light and Fast Organisation*

Tony Hsieh, *Delivering Happiness: Profits, Passion and Purpose*

Dr Amantha Imber, *The Creativity Formula*

Frans Johannsen, *The Medici Effect*

Phil Knight, *Shoe Dog*

Patrick Lencioni, *The Five Dysfunctions of a Team*

L. David Marquet, *Turn the Ship Around*

General Stanley McChrystal, *Team of Teams*

Patty McCord, *Powerful: Building a Culture of Freedom and Responsibility*

Dr Martyn Newman, *Emotional Capitalists*

Scott E. Page, *The Diversity Bonus: How Great Teams Pay Off in the Knowledge Economy*

Dan Pink, *Drive*

Mary Shapiro, *HBR Guide to Leading Teams*

Richard Sheridan, *Joy Inc.*

Chade-Meng Tan, *Search Inside Yourself*

Ashlee Vance, *Elon Musk*

Gary Vaynerchuck, *#AskGaryVee: One Entrepreneur's Take on Leadership, Social media and Self-awareness*

Benjamin & Rosamund Stone Zander, *The Art of Possibility*

ABOUT COLIN

Colin D. Ellis is an award-winning international speaker, best-selling author and renowned leadership and culture expert who works with organisations around the world to help them transform the way they get things done.

Able to draw on more than 30 years of public and private sector leadership experience, Colin peppers his sessions with anecdotes, statistics, practical insights and plenty of humour to ensure that attendees are engaged and laughing!

He gets people talking by encouraging people to be the best version of themselves and to create teams and communities they can be proud of. There's often an assumption that everyone knows how to do this and that it's easy to do. This is not the case. All too often people's behaviours don't match the positions they hold.

Colin is originally from Liverpool in the UK and now lives in — and travels frequently from — Melbourne, Australia. He is also known for his snappy dressing, sense of humour and love of karaoke.

He runs highly successful culture programs and delivers memorable speeches. More information can be found on these at www.culturefix.xyz

INDEX

Lightning Source UK Ltd.
Milton Keynes UK
UKHW050203070919
349257UK00005B/18/P

9 780730 371496